Human-Computer Interactions in Museums

Synthesis Lectures on Human-Centred Informatics

Editor

John M. Carroll, *Penn State University*

Human-Centred Informatics (HCI) is the intersection of the cultural, the social, the cognitive, and the aesthetic with computing and information technology. It encompasses a huge range of issues, theories, technologies, designs, tools, environments, and human experiences in knowledge work, recreation and leisure activity, teaching and learning, and the potpourri of everyday life. The series publishes state-of-the-art syntheses, case studies, and tutorials in key areas. It shares the focus of leading international conferences in HCI.

Human-Computer Interactions in Museums
Eva Hornecker and Luigina Ciolfi

Encounters with HCI Pioneers: A Personal History and Photo Journal
Ben Shneiderman

Social Media and Civic Engagement: History, Theory, and Practice
Scott P. Robertson

The Art of Interaction: What HCI Can Learn from Interactive Art
Ernest Edmonds

Representation, Inclusion, and Innovation: Multidisciplinary Explorations
Clayton Lewis

Research in the Wild
Yvonne Rogers and Paul Marshall

Designing for Gesture and Tangible Interaction
Mary Lou Maher and Lina Lee

From Tool to Partner: The Evolution of Human-Computer Interaction
Jonathan Grudin

Qualitative HCI Research: Going behind the Scenes
Ann Blandford, Dominic Furnies, and Stephann Makri

© Springer Nature Switzerland AG 2022

Reprint of original edition © Morgan & Claypool 2019

Human-Computer Interactions in Museums
Eva Hornecker and Luigina Ciolfi

ISBN: 978-3-031-01097-2   paperback
ISBN: 978-3-031-00205-2   hard cover
ISBN: 978-3-031-02225-8   ebook

DOI 10.1007/978-3-031-02225-8

A Publication in the Springer series
SYNTHESIS LECTURES ON HUMAN-CENTRED INFORMATICS, #42

Series Editor: John M. Carroll, Penn State University
Series ISSN: 1946-7680 Print   1946-7699 Electronic

Human-Computer Interactions in Museums

Eva Hornecker
Bauhaus-Universität Weimar, Germany

Luigina Ciolfi
Sheffield Hallam University, UK

SYNTHESIS LECTURES ON HUMAN-CENTRED INFORMATICS #42

ABSTRACT

Museums have been a domain of study and design intervention for Human-Computer Interaction (HCI) for several decades. However, while resources providing overviews on the key issues in the scholarship have been produced in the fields of museum and visitor studies, no such resource as yet existed within HCI. This book fills this gap and covers key issues regarding the study and design of HCIs in museums. Through an on-site focus, the book examines how digital interactive technologies impact and shape galleries, exhibitions, and their visitors. It consolidates the body of work in HCI conducted in the heritage field and integrates it with insights from related fields and from digital heritage practice. Processes of HCI design and evaluation approaches for museums are also discussed. This book draws from the authors' extensive knowledge of case studies as well as from their own work to provide examples, reflections, and illustrations of relevant concepts and problems.

This book is designed for students and early career researchers in HCI or Interaction Design, for more seasoned investigators who might approach the museum domain for the first time, and for researchers and practitioners in related fields such as heritage and museum studies or visitor studies. Designers who might wish to understand the HCI perspective on visitor-facing interactive technologies may also find this book useful.

KEYWORDS

HCI, museums, interaction design, digital heritage, heritage technology, museum installation, informal learning

Contents

Acknowledgements

We wish to acknowledge the support of Diane Cerra and Jack Carroll at Morgan & Claypool, the valuable feedback of the reviewers Rachel Clarke and Michael Twidale, and the contribution of the illustrators Caroline Claisse and Katharina Bartholomäus. We give our thanks to the people who kindly granted permission to use their images for this book: Gabriela Avram, Loraine Clarke, Nick Dulake, Jane Finnis and Culture24, Valérie Maquil, Christian Moll, Holger Schnädelbach, and Dirk vom Lehn. Luigina Ciolfi wishes to thank Gabriela Avram, Daniela Petrelli, Nick Dulake, Laura Maye, Mark Marshall, Marc McLoughlin, and Liam Bannon for all the joint work done together in museums over many years; thanks also to Jenny Kidd for the many extensive discussions about digital heritage that contributed to the development of this book. Eva Hornecker thanks Loraine Clarke and the MeSch project partners for the joint work on cultural heritage and museums.

Introduction

With the proliferation of technology being utilised in museums, museums have become a fertile research ground for Human-Computer Interaction (HCI) research and technology deployment. Museums are places for the exploration of ideas and the creative display of artefacts and information resources. Also, in aiming to attract visitors and to be seen as innovative and modern, museums often experiment with new ways of presentation. Because of this, they often are among the first venues for novel interactive technologies to be utilised and experienced by the general public (e.g., the first multi-touch tables), and can be a great testbed for trialing such technologies. Furthermore, museums provide a space other than research labs where a substantial number of users can be studied as they interact with digital devices and content. Being semi-public environments, they enable this by still making it possible for researchers to manage and control such trials.

All these reasons make museums and galleries an attractive context for HCI research. Moreover, it has become easier to generate computer-supported interactions due to the availability of archived digital content and supporting infrastructures for digitization and digital content management that can interface directly with digital interpretation means.

On a more general level, museums have been an important domain to be studied within HCI from the point of view of challenging assumptions with the notion of "use" and "interaction": some early studies captured and argued for the need to consider nuanced phenomena of interaction such as "legitimate peripheral participation," and the importance of social and collaborative interaction around digital systems. In this respect, museums have been key to the historical evolution of HCI as a discipline.

There has been a lot of recent work in related areas: "virtual museums" (which exist mainly online, but for some institutions are becoming digital extensions to "brick and mortar" museums—as well as archives and libraries—in order to widen their audience and complement physical exhibitions), digital humanities (usually data-based, including digitised text, images, 3D models, etc.), and supporting curation and data management for heritage archives.

However, in this book we focus on visitor interaction *within* physical museums. Our goal is to provide an introduction to this field for researchers and students new to this field of work, where relevant literature is otherwise dispersed across disciplines and practices.

The focus on visitors is important from our point of view so as to present a human-centred perspective on the challenges of adopting and using digital technologies in the heritage sector for interpretation and engagement purposes. We also wish to consolidate the body of work in HCI conducted in the heritage field, and integrate it with insights from related fields and from digital heritage practice. As our focus lies on visitor interactions in museums, we will not discuss at length other forms of digital strategy that heritage institutions adopt, such as social media or crowdsourcing campaigns mainly aimed at online engagement with visitors and other communities of interest.

We do, however, discuss the relationship between HCI researchers and museums as organisations, in terms of their attitudes, practices, policies, strategies, and expertise. No two museums are the same when it comes to how they engage their visitors and present their collections. In-house expertise can also be varied. Here, we shall usually employ the term "curators" for the cultural heritage professionals who decide what goes into an exhibition, and how the overall narrative or message is to be conveyed. Nevertheless, this is a complex professional category, including figures trained in archival science, archaeology, and other sciences relevant to the collection (e.g., history, but also biology and material science), or conservation, but also in museology, pedagogy, communication, and design. The expertise and knowledge that each museum offers is an important aspect to consider when designing interactive exhibitions. Besides curators, for example, there will be interpretation officers who develop textual resources, information panels, and self-guided tours, staff with a more pedagogical background who organise activity packs for schools and special activities or events for families, marketing experts dedicated to reaching out and engaging new audiences, and sometimes technical staff knowledgeable about digital platforms and tools. The role of HCI experts might therefore vary and need to be negotiated differently according to the skills, knowledge, and roles present.

We, the authors of this book, have accumulated 35 years of experience in this field when adding together our respective track records, and have worked on 12 major funded projects (and various small projects with students) involving a variety of heritage institutions and professionals from several countries. We come from overlapping and complementary backgrounds. Hornecker has a more HCI, evaluation-oriented perspective, with a focus on visitor engagement and informal learning; Ciolfi comes from a humanities-oriented and social science perspective, and specialises in participatory approaches to design. Both of us study the social and collaborative context of museum technologies, have worked on the tangible and embodied aspects of museum technologies, and proposed approaches to their design that take into account the material and embodied aspects of experiencing heritage. In addition, we have collaborated on a major EU project aimed at exploring physical-digital interactions in museums and enabling museum professionals to author installations themselves.

In supervising students doing HCI research related to museums and in reviewing and evaluating countless papers and proposals on these topics, we had come to realise that there is no single core resource for getting started in this field. We hope that this book will fill this gap. We are writing this book mainly for students and early career researchers in HCI or Interaction Design, but we believe that it will be useful also for more seasoned investigators who might approach the museum domain for the first time, and for researchers and practitioners in related fields such as heritage and museum studies or visitor studies, as well as designers, who might wish to understand the HCI body of work and perspective on interactive museum technologies and to engage with development and evaluation of visitor-facing interactive technologies.

In the chapters to follow, we mention various examples, but these are by no means all those that exist in relation to a certain topic. Rather, we selected representative instances that either yield important contributions in advancing the field, or that are particularly illustrative. We also refer liberally to our own work, as we know intimately how it addressed core issues. Our reliance on projects, institutions, and locations that we know by virtue of our personal experience means that a majority of examples in the book refer to work done in Northern Europe and North America. We have extensively researched both research and practice beyond these geographical areas and included mentions of work beyond these geographical boundaries. Despite this, we are conscious that a strong focus on Europe and North America remains. This can also be due to more established traditions of digital museum applications in these regions where museums have been open to experimentation for longer and have therefore led to several pioneering projects.

We are aware that in fields such as HCI and interactive technologies, innovations and advancements of the state of the art occur rapidly. While some of our examples might age a little as the book ages, we are confident that they will remain effective examples for illustrating key concepts, approaches, and concerns, as well as showcase of the history HCI in museums.

Readers should note that this is not a research methods or HCI handbook, as we only touch upon the role of certain models and methods in the context of evaluating or designing interactive technologies in museums. For more in-depth information, readers should refer to foundational HCI literature and to the research methods literature—as each model, method, or approach, especially with evaluation techniques, requires careful preparation and training.

OVERVIEW OF CHAPTERS

Chapter 1 discusses key themes relevant for understanding the field, including the institutional context of museums, practical and professional concerns of heritage professionals, situational characteristics of the museum visit, visitor characteristics and motivations, and much more. In this chapter, we try to provide an overview of central discussions and insights from the literature on visitor studies, heritage studies and informal learning in museums.

Chapter 2 investigates what we term "interaction frames": that is, different configurations of devices, input and output mechanisms, and the relationship of interaction with the physical context of the museum. We discuss standalone installations, assemblies of interconnected components distributed over a site, and mobile interactions. We also discuss different types of augmentation, such as embodied and embedded interactions, extended reality (including Virtual and Augmented Reality), and multisensory interactions.

Chapter 3 discusses approaches for visitor participation and the inclusion of visitor-generated content and contributions in exhibitions. In recent years, there has been increased effort to adopt participatory approaches, which give visitors a voice in the design of exhibitions, enabling them to comment or generate content for others to see. We discuss approaches from bespoke interactions on site in museums and the use of crowdsourcing and social media platforms in relation to gallery visits.

Chapter 4 gives an overview of development approaches and methods in the creation of museum installations. We discuss the role of user-centred design and how to adapt it to the museum context, and of participatory approaches, where either visitors or cultural heritage professionals (or in some cases both) are crucially involved in the design process. We also discuss the growing area of Do-It-Yourself tools that allow cultural heritage professionals and other non-technology experts to build interactive installations. Finally, we discuss some critical concerns that need to be kept in mind during the development process, regardless of its approach.

Chapter 5 deals with evaluation approaches and techniques for evaluating interactive installations. We discuss mixed-method vs. single-method studies, providing examples of how methods can complement each other, and then discuss various popular methods, from timing and tracking approaches, interaction logs, over questionnaires, interviews, and observational approaches, to fine-grained video and conversation analysis. We also discuss methods aimed at assessing visitor learning and conclude with pointers on evaluation from a practitioner's perspective.

Finally, Chapter 6 touches on how ongoing changes in how museums position themselves challenge and iinfluence how the design of museum technologies should be approached, and how people's evolving relationship with technology in their daily life changes expectations and behaviour. We return to the tension between whether museums should be seen as a space for experimentation for HCI or whether they should be treated as application partners that have their own requirements and goals, where ideally HCI research work contributes to museums' long-term strategies and development. We conclude with our own lessons learned over the course of our career, doing research in and with museums, all of which writing this book gave us a welcome chance to reflect upon.

CHAPTER 1

Understanding the Context: Key Themes for Visitor Interaction in Museums

A number of factors influence the potential success of museum installations and digital interactivity. Similar to other areas of Human-Computer Interaction (HCI), design needs to be aware of the characteristics of the context of use, which influence its fit with the setting and with the institution, adoption and appropriation of the technology, and user reactions. A common mistake is to think of interactive technology for museums in isolation, or to think that technology from other contexts (e.g., the classroom) can directly be imported into a museum. However, just as with any other application context, we need to be aware of user characteristics and motivations, user expectations, the physical context of use, the social context of use, task demands (or situational requirements), as well as organisational and socio-cultural issues related to museums as organisations and to the practice/field of museum management and curatorship (issues that include the ethos and mission of a museum, the visitor experience it aims to deliver, the digital expertise of museum professionals, etc.).

Museums nowadays are identifying and identified not only as authoritative sources of knowledge and safe repositories of heritage holdings, but also as places for discussion, mutual learning, and even empathy. From the "New Museology" of the late 1980s and 1990s advocating museums as places for cultural discourse, to the "participatory" trends in museums today, these trends have meant that research and practice on digital technologies for museums have also evolved.

Dimensions of Visitor Experience.

Falk and Dierking (1992) posit that visitor experience is influenced by physical context (architecture, physical exhibit design, exhibited objects), social context (shared visits, presence of other visitors, interactions with staff), and personal context (motivations, preferences, knowledge). At the same time, visitors' active engagement in and with museums has physical, emotional, intellectual, and social dimensions (Perry, 2012). New trends in visitor studies emphasise multisensory and emotional engagement as well as the sociality of museum experience (Falk and Dierking, 2013; Levent and Pascual, 2014; Bedford, 2014; Perry, 2012; Macdonald, 2007).

As the discourse on museums becomes richer and more diverse, this influences empirical work on how visitors interact, learn, and experience museums as well as practical work in exhibit and exhibition design. Museums are increasingly conceptualised as active memory sites, rather than repositories that are approached for educational purposes: representing personal values, activating (and either amplifying or contrasting) social and individual memories (Kavanagh, 2000). Further discourses that gain importance thus include, for example, the debate on how museums and exhibitions communicate ideas and values, exemplified by the #museumsarenotneutral (Twitter hashtag, where many museum professionals shared their experience). This highlights how knowledge and heritage holdings may be classified and presented from a limited perspective (such as eurocentric, or colonialist), misrepresenting or silencing others and frequently objectifying or excluding the people whose heritage is on display (Macdonald Intro, 2006; Sandell and Nightingale, 2012). Museums can carry deep (and potentially unsettling) political and cultural frames, and they should be treated as such.

This is not a museum studies book, and thus we are not going to give an overview of all important debates in museology and heritage practice. Nevertheless, it is important to flag some key trends/debates as they affect HCI research. Museums are a rich, complex, and often contested environment, and the HCI researchers intending to work in this context must be aware of its key discourses.

1.1   THE MUSEUM—BUT IS THERE SUCH A THING AS "THE MUSEUM"?

While the first museums (intended as curated displays of artefacts) originated from private collections that were more of a "Wunderkammer" (cabinet of curiosities) and simply showcased remarkable or mysterious objects for their own sake, museums as institutions aimed at a public audience (and which became an established part of public life in the 19th century) always wanted to educate as well as archive and protect. This was usually related to an agenda: for instance many public museums in European countries were established in order to celebrate and cohere national identity at a time of expanding colonial endeavour, showing national heritage and history, or showcasing the nation's international role. Since then, museums have two major roles in society: serving public education as well as contributing to culture preservation and conservation (and related research). In recent years, this has extended to, for example, contributing to community development (Ciolfi et al., 2018) and cultural industries, with an increasing set of marketable assets and activities, including those related to tourism and entertainment.

While it is tempting to think of "the museum" as such as one type of institution, there are different types (or genres) of museums. These types of museums tend to look different and have a different base of visitors; furthermore, expectations of visitors of what to expect and how to behave there are based on the genre and on the way each museum presents itself, just like people behave differently at a techno gig, a punk concert or a classical recital. These evoke so-called "behaviour settings". Bell argues that such "visit rituals, along with other factors, including the constraints of funding and entrance fees result in a variety of museum ecologies, with science and technology museums on the one side of the spectrum and art museums or galleries on the other" (Bell, 2002).

Figure 1.1: Different types of museums not only house different types of exhibition items and appeal to different audiences, but also constitute divergent genres in terms of rules and expectations of how to behave (art museum, science museum, natural history museum) (illustration by Katharina Bartholomäus).

Science museums tend to have various machines for visitors to use (Sandifer, 2003). Famous examples include the Munich Deutsches Museum (a pioneer of this kind of institution since the early 20th century), the San Francisco Exploratorium, and the Miraikan (the National Museum of Emerging Science and Innovation) in Tokyo, Japan. Interactive installations are purpose-built to let visitors experience and help them understand scientific phenomena. Science museums are often visited by families with children, and visitors do expect to be able to touch and manipulate things as they will have experienced this in other science museums. Moreover, the visual design used in such museums communicates a "hands-on" culture—the museum will be packed with machines with big handles and cranks, there are no ropes or barriers around installations, the building and installations tend to be colourful, and the museum will be noisy, due to visitors as well as exhibitions. Dedicated "children's museums" are very similar in style to science museums, and share a lot of their characteristics.

Art museums or galleries (such as Amsterdam Rijksmuseum, the New York MOMA, or the Louvre, to mention just a few world-famous examples), as well as archeological museums (Cairo's Museum of Egyptian Antiquities, the National Archaeological Museum in Athens, or as an example for smaller collections, the Petrie Museum of Egyptian Archaeology in London), tend to be at the other extreme. In particular for the arts, the "white cube" architecture, where visitors experience each artwork in isolation, is very typical. The exhibits are intended to be seen from relative distance. People have learned that art is precious and delicate, and they are not allowed to get too close, not to mention touch it, and that art is to be "appreciated" and contemplated. People behave almost as in a church—wandering around, standing still to watch, and being silent, so as not to disturb others. An effect of this culturally learned behaviour is that even if there happens to be artwork and installations that are meant to be touched and interacted with, many visitors will not try to or will hesitate, needing strong encouragement and reassurance that any other behaviour is appropriate. Arts and archeological museums tend to be visited by a more mature visitor demographic, although they are also popular for school visits as part of the educational curriculum. In this case, pupils and students will likely behave in ways that are very different from a family visit to a hands-on museum, and most likely will be strictly supervised so that the general rules of behaviour in these spaces are upheld.

Next to these two extremes, many other types of museums exist. Museums of technology (such as the Powerhouse Museum in Sydney and the Technical Museum in Vienna), for example, sit halfway between the two, showing many historic artefacts but also often demonstrating their inner workings either with old machinery that is still working or with replicas that can be interacted with. They tend to have a very mixed visitorship across all ages, being popular with young children as well as with adults. History museums (as well as museums of natural history), like arts museums, will often show historical artefacts behind glass, illustrating and discussing, for example, a city's history or the life of a historical character. There are also history museums that focus on communicating ideas and values (e.g., the history of apartheid, race segregation, Jewish history and persecution, women's rights, etc.) and will combine artefacts with text, video/image material, and aim also at emotional and empathic engagement. Many of these encourage reflection on ethical and moral values, aiming to build understanding and learning through emotional engagement. Examples include the International Slavery Museum in Liverpool, the Guernica Peace Museum in Guernica, Spain, the Imperial War Museum London, the House of Slaves Museum and Memorial in Dakar, Senegal, and the Kigali Genocide Memorial in Rwanda. When museums deal with sensitive historical issues, racial or societal divisions, or historical and ongoing conflict, interaction design and research in this area of interpretation requires respectful awareness of such sensitive agendas.

Some museums are hard to categorise in this respect, as they combine different sections, including national history, art, local history, and heritage. Examples include New Zealand's Te Papa Tongarewa and the Glasgow Kelvingrove museum in Scotland. A few art museums have invested in developing interactive "companions" to their more traditional displays in the form of dedicated galleries or exhibitions where a more hands-on relationship with art objects and antiquities can be developed (such as for example the Cleveland Art Museum's ARTLENS Gallery), or through other hands-on activities to take place in the galleries, such as art workshops and poetry recitals, aimed at changing the general atmosphere and to encouraging a more active relationship with the collections. Arts museums that encourage a more hands-on behaviour are still unusual, therefore visitors will need encouragement to play by different rules. While such "companion spaces" allow a more hands-on relationship (in particular when aimed at children), these spaces are usually demarcated physically and visually, indicating that different rules of behaviour apply.

Other types of museums/heritage sites to be visited include house museums (where the entire building, its contents, and sometimes even its grounds, are what is on display, e.g., the Jane Austen's House Museum), and open air museums (e.g., entire villages or larger environments and landscapes), where frequently old crafts practices or everyday activities are re-enacted (for instance, Skansen in Stockholm, Sweden—the oldest of this kind—Bunratty Castle and Folk Park in Ireland, the Village Museum in Dar es Salaam, Tanzania, and Seurasaari Open-Air Museum in Helsinki, Finland). In historic houses and open-air museums, the visitor is literally immersed within the exhibit. Any technological intervention thus has to integrate into the overall narrative, and, frequently also with the aesthetics, atmosphere and appearance of the site.

An orthogonal approach to differentiation would be between small, and usually low-budget, museums typically concentrating on local history and everyday life, and well-funded larger (and often internationally renowned) museums, some of which may be managed by commercial corporations and others by public agencies, all of which operate according to different economic rules and with different aims (Macdonald, 2006).

These differences have profound implications for both designing and evaluating digital museum installations. While it may be obvious to consider demographics (designing for children versus older adults), visitor expectations and behaviour patterns also play a role. For example, whereas it is really hard to prevent visitors to a science museum from touching an exhibit (and these need to be extremely sturdy), in an art museum, a lot of effort has to be invested for communicating via the exhibit design that this may be allowed and even encouraged. This also extends to the kinds of behaviours and activities that visitors perceive to be appropriate. Horn et al. (2012) observed some adults discouraging their children from playing a touchscreen installation game in a natural history museum, saying things like: "We're not here to play games". They recommend communicating the educational value of such games and to provide parents with a role in the activity.

Moreover, the visual aesthetics and style of the overall environment need to be considered in design. Installations producing ambient sound to people entering a room in an art gallery might work well (or might be considered too noisy), but would be completely drowned out from the buzz and noise typical for science museums. Contemporary exhibition design (Bruckner, 2011) frequently aims at designing an overall holistic experience, using elements from *scenography*, a practical discipline that originally focused on theatre stage design. Scenography uses professional theatrical lighting, colour and sound design, architecture (spatial imagery and spatial dramaturgy), and object design to create immersive atmosphere. It aims to create aesthetic impact via sensual experience while also supporting the content and message of the exhibition. Some professional designers that specialise in exhibition design describe their work as scenography, and most are trained in either visual design and/or architecture.

Furthermore, the role of original artefacts within exhibitions/museums varies. While some exhibitions rely largely on interactive installations that give access to content, in object-focused exhibitions interactives tend to play more of a supporting role. While well-designed digital installations can increase the time spent in exhibitions and with individual exhibits (Gammon and Burch, 2008; Economou, 2010), the "absorbing power" of screen displays can also overshadow the experience of real artefacts and objects in those cases where they should be the main focus of a visit (Economou, 2010).

1.2   WHO ARE THE USERS: VISITOR DEMOGRAPHICS AND MOTIVATIONS

As we mentioned, different types of museums tend to attract different visitor demographics. Moreover, a single museum might attract several fairly distinct visitor groups; for example, the Museum of Transport in Glasgow, Scotland, is popular with families with children, schools (for field trips), older adults, and also tourists. It is good practice in designing museum interactivity to determine its target group(s), so as to address specific visitor types through the design. Knowing the most important target group(s) and audiences is also essential for testing and evaluating (see Hornecker and Nicol, 2011).

Furthermore, group constellations are to be considered: for example, will adults visit the museum largely by themselves, as couples, or in larger groups, or will children visit a museum mostly as part of large (school) groups or with family? The design of an installation aimed at children can provide a role for parents to take on (e.g., as planner of activity, or surveiller of progress), ensuring they do not get bored, can interact productively with their children, and can scaffold children's learning. Testing and evaluation can also take account of this: for example, it would be unrealistic to expect toddlers to be left completely to their own devices by parents, while older children might be left free to explore on their own in the museum's safe environment. Furthermore, given that families often visit with several children and that adults will also most likely visit as part of pairs and small groups, it might be good to know whether multi-user interaction is possible or whether observers would get bored while a companion is interacting (Hornecker and Nicol, 2011).

Falk and Dierking (2013) raised the point that museum visitors engage in "free-choice learning", which is fundamentally different to, for example, school learning, in that visitors learn what they want to learn, and do not follow an external agenda. They follow their own interest, and may even decide not to learn and rather just seek entertainment. Free-choice learning subsumes all kinds of self-directed information-seeking activities, where people aim to increase their understanding and satisfy their curiosity. Visitors bring with them their own agenda and experiences, which will influence what learning experiences they might seek, how they want to learn, what they are interested in, etc. Thus, there has been a trend in visitor studies toward accepting that visitors are active interpreters (Macdonald, 2007). While learning is an important motivation for visiting a museum, it is not by all means the only one.

Falk (2009) distinguishes between different types of experience that museum visitors seek, resulting in five "experience types": explorers, who are motivated by curiosity; facilitators, who want to facilitate the experience of others; experience-seekers (e.g., tourists) looking for a special experience; professionals and hobbyists who seek to deepen their knowledge or engage in their passion; and rechargers, for whom the visit has a restorative or contemplative aspect. It is important to note that these are not mutually exclusive categories (Davies and Heath, 2014), as one person can be one or another depending on the situation and mood, and the type of museum and its theme, or one person might seek to address multiple needs.

In the *Selinda* model, Perry (2012) distinguishes six motivators: the desire for communication (or exchange of ideas); for curiosity to be raised and satisfied; the need to feel confident; the desire to challenge oneself; to feel in charge and in control; and for play. Pekarik et al. (1999) discusses four types of satisfying experiences for museum visitors, based on interview and survey data: visitors enjoy object experiences (seeing rare objects or the "real thing", being moved by beauty, imagining owning or interacting with objects); cognitive experiences (i.e., learning, understanding more); introspective experiences (imagining other places and times, feeling belonging or a connection, reminiscing); and social experiences (spending time with others, seeing one's children learn). Different types of museums as well as exhibit topics tend to engender some experience types more than others. Bedford (2014) discusses resonance and wonder: visitors being moved by "'the power of the displayed object" as a "numinous experience", which expands the notion of object experience with transcendent aspects. There is also evidence that visitors tend to be attracted to either ideas (knowledge, questions), objects (artefacts), or people (the lives of others), later extended with physical (sensorial engagement or movement) (IPOP-model). Pekarik et al. (2014) discuss how text displays can be used to attract people, that e.g., have an idea- or object focus, and nudge them toward to the object on display.

Overall, it is important to be aware of the demographics and characteristics of visitors when designing interactive installations, however this needs to be considered in context: in some past HCI work, designed interactions were based on establishing typologies of users (e.g., tourists will want A, students will want B), which were expected to behave and interact in a certain (and consistent) way. This approach is not likely to lead to effective designs, given that (as we saw) the motivations people have to visit a museum may change depending on many factors, and these may highly vary. Designing interactive visitor experiences must allow for a degree of flexibility, and of freedom for visitors to adjust the experience (and related content) to their own evolving interests.

Other attempts to categorise visitor types have been based not on demographics, but on the behavioural aspects of visits (dwell time, physical path followed in a exhibition, gaze, orientation, etc.) (Serrell, 1997). Such behavioural aspects as indicators of engagement or content preferences can also be short-sighted: for example, assuming a certain visitor's degree of interest on the basis of the time he or she spends around a certain exhibition. There is evidence that onlooking does not correspond to lower interest, for example as "legitimate peripheral participation" is an important aspect of group interaction around exhibits, representing effective coordination dynamics within a group and not different degrees of interest or engagement (Heath, vom Lehn, and Osborne, 2005).

1.3   PERSONALISATION: HOW MUSEUMS ADDRESS DIFFERENT VISITOR TYPES

Due to the fact that most museums target more than one demographic, and that identifying and targeting audience segments can lead to repeat visits and long-term engagement, museums dedicate much effort to offer personalised visiting experiences. Basic approaches to personalisation include offering different activities to different visitor groups, such as activity sheets to make children's visits more playful, structured visit packages for school groups (which can include guided tours on certain themes, such as history or geography, and a follow-up hands-on activity), and handling sessions or in-gallery talks for adult "enthusiasts". Specific approaches to personalisation are deployed to the design of content accompanying the visit: from guides and floor plans in various languages to support visitors from different cultures, to recommended visitor paths for those interested in a certain artist, or historical period, scientific theme, or for those who have limited time to spend at the museum (particularly at large museums) to choose between a 1-hour tour, 3-hour, or 5-hour tour.

Digital technologies have been employed to deliver personalised experiences in several ways, and sometimes adopting automated mechanisms for personalisation (to varying degrees of success). However, it must be noted how museums deliver a certain degree of personalisation well before any digital technology is adopted, and that this is often successful by virtue of enabling visitors in the same group to enjoy slightly unique experiences (for example by carrying guiding materials on different themes), as described, for example, in the case studies included in Samis and Michaelson (2016). The issue of providing effective ways to personalisation via digital technologies is one of the main avenues of research and practice around mobile interactions, and we will discuss it further in Section 2.1.2.

1.4   SOCIAL CONTEXT: SOCIAL AND COLLABORATIVE INTERACTIONS

The museum situation is inherently social—visitors frequently come to spend time with family, children, or friends, hoping the visit to be a memorable shared experience (Kelly et al., 2004; Heath and vom Lehn, 2002; Perry, 2012), may interact with strangers, or at least are indirectly affected by the presence of other visitors (vom Lehn et al., 2007; Hornecker, 2010). The social context is identified as one of the core aspects of the visitor experience (Falk, Dierking, and Adams, 2006; Perry, 2012; Kelly et al., 2004), but is often still ignored in (institutional) evaluation approaches (Davies and Heath, 2014).

Taking account of the social nature of museum visits is important in the design of digital interactions. Research in Computer Supported Cooperative Work (CSCW) revealed how requirements for group work can conflict with requirements for individual work (Gutwin and Greenberg, 2002). Groups attend an exhibit together, and might get bored if only one person can use it, with nothing to entertain and engage the others therewith. We have already mentioned group constellations, and recent museum studies literature has highlighted the role of family and parent-child interactions, with parents explaining, pointing out things, and asking questions, guiding children's thinking and attention while looking at objects (Kelly et al., 2004; Sanford et al., 2007). We can explicitly design for group interaction, where several people can be active, or can take on supportive roles and remain part of the conversation if the interaction is easily observable, e.g., deciding together on the course of action even if only one person is at the controls. Based on their observations of an interactive multitouch table, Block et al. (2015) advise to design for small groups, in particular for pairs (as these tend to spend the most time at exhibits), but at the same time to ensure a meaningful single-user experience given that 30% of visitors interact on their own. Snibbe and Raffle (2009), on the basis of extended experience in developing interactive camera/projector exhibits, recommend designing scalable interactions that become richer as more people interact with them.

Figure 1.2: The museum visit is usually a social experience, comprising playful activities as well as discussion and joint admiration or reminiscence within groups of family or friends (photographs by Eva Hornecker).

Furthermore, visitors tend to observe other visitors, which can remove the suspense or surprise of interactive exhibits that only have one outcome to interaction. However this phenomenon can also be used productively in exhibit design, for example, by turning the activity of visitors into something other visitors can enjoy to observe, where onlooking is informative or entertaining, and fosters discussion. Sometimes, the presence of other visitors can help to make it easier to understand how an exhibit works (if it is accidentally triggered and this can be seen by onlookers) (Heath, vom Lehn, and Osborne, 2005), or seeing others use it can demonstrate that the exhibit is fun or valuable, while previous users also serve as role-model for how to interact (Hornecker and Stifter, 2006a).

The presence of other visitors can also mean that visitors leave an exhibit mid-stage, or that somebody might join them mid-stage, with overlap between different visitor groups being common (cf. Block et al., 2015). This means, that some visitors might arrive at a deserted installation while it is not in its initial state, while others may observe an ongoing interaction process, but might have missed crucial cues as to what this is about and what to do. Exhibit design thus needs to design for this, which is harder to accomplish with physical designs that cannot have a reset button. Traditional hands-on exhibits often have a reset button, and many digital interactives utilise a timeout to restart. This is more difficult with tangible objects being part of an installation, which would need to be manually cleared or individually reset. Good exhibition design takes account of this and aims to ensure that visitors know what to do regardless of in which state they encounter the exhibit.

Moreover, social interactions around exhibits have been found to contribute to learning, since learning does not just occur by virtue of the exhibit communicating to a visitor, but can take place between group members. Meaning and sensemaking are actively constructed and frequently constructed and elaborated in conversation (Ellenbogen et al., 2004; Gutwill and Allen, 2010). In particular, current models of museum learning emphasise that it is dialogic, constructivist, and contextual (Falk and Dierking, 2000; Perry, 2012).

1.5   ACTIVITY CONTEXT—THE SOCIO-CONTEXTUAL SETTING

While there are elements of learning occurring when people visit museums, and curators do hope for learning to occur (and many visitors want to learn), museums are a place of "free-choice learning" (Falk and Dierking, 2000; Falk, Dierking, and Adams, 2006), where visitors decide *what* they are interested in and may reject or not be interested in what curators define as desired learning outcomes. In particular, unlike at school, visitors are not a "captive audience".

For interactive installations to be successful, they need to have what Allen (2004) refers to as "immediate apprehendability": in other words, visitors need to quickly grasp how to interact. Bitgood (2013) adds another component with his Attention-Value model: if visitors can (easily) perceive an exhibit or installation to provide high value, they are more likely to pay attention to it. Visitors will weigh off effort (i.e., cost), for example of reading labels (or of interacting) to the perceived value of paying attention. These factors crucially determine the attracting power of interactives in an exhibition, where there is a plentitude of potential value-providing objects that visitors can focus on, which all compete for their attention. Value is thus relative to the alternatives available. If interaction is difficult or does not provide an immediate reward, most visitors will quickly give up and leave, unless the final reward is very high and clearly visible. Visitors will quickly migrate toward more evident "rewards" in sight. It is usually far easier to reduce the cost of paying attention (e.g., reducing the length of text on labels and information panels) than to increase the benefit, as the latter requires creating content or outcomes of higher value.

This makes the testing of museum interactives difficult—while a traditional lab-based usability test will uncover hurdles for interaction and help improve the design per se, it is hard to predict whether visitors will approach the interactive, try it out, and see enough value to persist, or get distracted and attracted by other things in the vicinity. Devices or installations that are attractive for use at home or in school learning, or that are considered attractive when experienced without competition, may fail to attract attention or prolonged use when set out in a museum context (cf. Hornecker and Nicol, 2012). Furthermore, it is important to keep in mind that visitors are likely to wander off in the middle of interacting with an installation (even if is just because a group member wants to move on or is tired). Thus, long interaction sequences (comparable to video games) can be problematic. Horn et al. (2012) found that with multi-level games, visitors who then take over the free space are confused, since they face an advanced game level, having missed the introductory rounds. They recommend using only a limited number of levels, time-outs (for a restart), and easy manual ways to restart (which are not accidentally triggered).

1.6   THE ROLE OF CONTENT AND MUSEUM LEARNING

Besides of the type of museum, other factors impact what museums look like. Architecture is influenced by fashion trends, as is graphic design. Still, more importantly, choice of content, exhibition message, and approach taken to convey this message are usually decided upon by museum curators or other museum professionals such as interpretation officers (the staff dedicated to producing interpretation resources such as brochures, panels, textual descriptions, etc.) and might be refined by professional exhibit designers and companies.

Different types of museum or exhibition content and topics furthermore lend themselves to different types of design; for example, some exhibitions will be full of original objects, and in this case, the role of interactives will tend to be that of providing supporting information, including background context, triggering imagination, or allowing playful approaches, whereas other exhibition types will have only few artefacts to display, and will rely on images, text, and purpose-built installations to convey a topic or concept.

Historically, there has been a progression of didactic approaches prominent in museums, which was heavily influenced by the learning sciences. George Hein (1998) suggests a typology of pedagogical views (roughly chronological):

- *didactic expository*: communicating pre-decided knowledge and message, curators are in control of what visitors do, learn, and maybe even feel (transmission model, learning seen as passive reception);

- *stimulus-response*: repetition of activity, reward for correct answers, learning of facts (still similar to transmission model);

- *discovery framework*: enabling visitors to explore, with open-ended activities (prominent example: Exploratorium SF); and

- *constructivism*: open-ended narratives, enabling and encouraging visitors to make their own meaning, trying to connect with the visitors' experience that they bring in.

This progression moves from a transmission model (where the information and message to be learned is chosen upfront and evaluation of learning would assess this learning outcome) toward more constructivist and transactional models that view the visitor (or learner) as driving their own learning and interpretation, based on their experience and intentions (this view is related to the model of free-choice learning). While newer didactic models have become more dominant, it is still common to see exhibitions guided by a more traditional perspective where curators feel strongly about what visitors should learn, and that prioritise domain accuracy. These perspectives frequently clash when museums experiment with visitor-created content, e.g., through social media, where the actual contents of an exhibition and/or the information provided are curated by visitors or integrated by their contributions, which intrinsically entails giving up some curational control.

Falk and Dierking (e.g., Falk, Dierking, and Adams, 2006) warn that defining learning outcomes such as "visitors will learn/understand XYZ" does not account for free-choice learning and tends to be limited to cognitive outcomes. The design of exhibits should give more freedom to visitors to choose. Furthermore, a variety of learning and interpretation outcomes should be considered as equally valid: for example, enhancing skills, developing an interest, thinking about values, being empathic, being creative, developing awareness of a topic, or social learning. This is supported by the work of other heritage scholars arguing for the importance of all aspects of the visitor experience, including becoming emotional, feeling uncomfortable or upset, and identifying with the "voices" of an exhibition. The design of exhibits can explicitly underpin this, for example by using types of content such as witness accounts of historical facts (Arnold-Simine, 2013; Gokcigdem, 2016).

As an example, a museum visit might raise a teenager's awareness of the topic of racial discrimination and emphasise values of equality and democracy, potentially through an emotional experience, thus resulting in increased motivation to learn more about the topic. At the Centre for Civil and Human Rights in Atlanta, Georgia, visitors can take place in a life-size re-enactment of a sit-in protest of African-American college students against being excluded from being served lunch at a restaurant. Visitors can take the seat of a student protester and put their hands on the handprints placed on a countertop; they can hear people yelling and hitting the table, and feel their bar stool vibrating.

1.7   SPECIFIC NEEDS OF HERITAGE INSTITUTIONS

A major reason for introducing novel interactive installations into museums is often the assumption that this can attract new (often younger) audiences, as well as the desire to project an innovative, modern image of itself (rather than old-fashioned, or "stuffy"). The launch of large-scale, innovative installations furthermore draws media attention, which draws further visitors, as well as raising the museum's international profile. In addition, the politics of funding bodies and their agendas and policies frequently drive decision making in how and where technology is situated within the museum sector, and even with regard to which technology should be developed. For example, recent funding initiatives by the Arts and Humanities Research Council in the UK aimed at the cultural sector have put emphasis on "immersive" technologies such as Augmented and Virtual Reality. Similarly, the European Union has championed specific types of technologies through a number of multi-million funding programmes: from 3D and VR reconstruction, to mobile location-aware platforms, and pervasive media (such as in *The Disappearing Computer* flagship initiative 2001–2004).

Besides curators' aims for what visitors should "take home", a range of other factors influence the design and deployment of exhibits. These can be very pragmatic, relating to costs of purchase and upkeep, maintenance issues, and conservation demands (Maye et al., 2014). Maintenance is a core issue, as external funding often only covers the initial development and setup. Moreover, applications and computers need to be administered, e.g., requiring regular content or software updates as well as restarts (needing staff who can do this), and technology quickly gets out of date. Thus, technology-based exhibits tend to look dated much more quickly than others (e.g., a joystick is an old technology by today's standards, and visitors are not used to interacting with it anymore). Given that studies have shown that visitor satisfaction is severely hampered when large numbers of exhibits are out of order (Kollmann, 2007) and that this can affect a museum's perceived credibility, it can be a risky (and expensive) strategy to rely on a high number of interactives. And it is not only about non-working exhibits. Visitors may mis-perceive interactive exhibits as "broken", even if they do work, when attempts to use them fail because they are too difficult to use.

Economic considerations can relate to whether an exhibit is relevant to a museum's mission and the availability of funds and to subsequent resources needed for upkeep and management. Interactive exhibits in general are more costly to produce than static exhibits (West, 2004). This is because, often, new software and hardware must be designed, fabricated, and tested because of the need to stay up-to-date with technology (not to get outdated), and for operating and maintenance costs. Complexity, construction quality, medium chosen, labour and materials, theme, and scale of the exhibit influence cost. Moreover, if an entire exhibition is developed, predicting final costs may be difficult if design modifications need to be made during the process.

Rapid obsolescence of technology is a frequent issue. Some systems quickly look dated, might even lose any familiarity people have with them, and then become hard to use (e.g., interaction via trackballs). Moreover, hardware, software, and operating systems at some point become outdated, making it costly (or even impossible) to upgrade. In addition, frequent outsourcing of installation development creates additional problems, as there will not always be a maintenance contract, and curators often lack the expertise and access to update and modify contents or behaviours, thus being unable to change anything if the exhibition changes or if evaluations reveal problems that would need remedial interventions (Maye et al., 2014).

In addition, we have to take account of demands in terms of curation, conservation and archival work. A student project that augmented the (existing) reconstruction of a prehistoric grave (Panier et al., 2016) involved a complex negotiation of the design space with curators around conflicts of interest between technological options, conservation, archaeological curation, and visitor/interaction experience. In this case, anything that interfered with the appearance of the grave was prohibited, while the integrity of artefacts had to be ensured and protected from damage and decay, which excluded various ideas for the design or for the technology to be used. Many curators also have concerns that screens and high-tech installations may distract from the actual artefacts and feel that these cannot be replaced. While this is known to happen (more to be discussed in Chapter 2), nevertheless, there is strong motivation for integrating innovative technologies: museums want to be seen as up-to-date, meet visitors' expectations, and see novel installations as a means for attracting and maintaining audiences, as well as garnering publicity (McDermott et al., 2013; Maye et al., 2014). Furthermore, such technologies are believed to provide the ability to communicate materials that may be invisible, or difficult to integrate into exhibits by non-digital means.

Moreover, there are other "political" and organisational issues. These include what role museums and curators desire for themselves, and their overall mission, approach, and strategy. Interview studies reveal that curators are frequently concerned about loss of authority and control and their significance as shaping interpretation, or of the museum being "dumbed down'" (Disneyfication), if the visitor experience is at the centre of attention (Reussner, 2010). HCI researchers who want to do research in museums need to be aware of all these factors that can influence negotiations and partnerships with museum management and staff about the design of exhibits, the focus of user studies, and of how findings become interpreted. Moreover, there is often an inherent conflict between the desire to understand how exhibition design can be improved and the need of museums to report (positively) to funders about the success of an exhibition (Davies and Heath, 2014).

It is important not to make assumptions about how a museum operates and how visitors experience it on the basis of its "type" or of what worked for other museums. Museums are not only gatekeepers to get by: they also are active stakeholders in this relationship, as well as bringing in invaluable domain knowledge. Furthermore, assumptions should not be made about the expertise that a museum as an organisation might hold: due to the breadth of the museum and heritage practice field, there might be staff with significant experience of digital technologies and digital engagement. For all these reasons it is important to approach this as a journey of mutual learning, one that can benefit both sides. Otherwise, there is the risk that resulting installations lack institutional support (important for upkeep and for how these are integrated into the museum's activities, i.e., guided tours, etc.), do not integrate with the overall exhibition design and strategy, or that interest for longer-term collaborations dwindles if stakeholders see no benefit.

CHAPTER 2

Different Interaction Frames

Digital technologies for museums not only address different themes of a possible visit, as we saw in Chapter 1, and are not only deployed for varying exhibition settings, they can also be strikingly different in terms of which physical-digital interaction they afford and by which hardware and software set-up. This chapter presents key interaction frames to have been applied to digital interventions in museums, and points out their main characteristics and issues relating to the visitor experience. With "interaction frame" we refer to the way in which the interactive experience is articulated in terms of type(s) of: device; input and output mechanisms; and relationship with the physical context of the museum and with other contextual factors, such as the presence of others. However, there is a certain degree of overlap and blending, particularly when considering the type of content each platform can support and the domain where it operates. Aware of this overlap, we distinguish these categories of interaction frames for illustrative and analytical purposes. Furthermore, to illustrate each category we refer to a number of examples. These are not exhaustive by any means, and we include them as selected representative cases of important features of each analytical category.

There is naturally a "historical" evolution in the platforms and devices deployed in museums: while in the early days of museum technologies standalone kiosks were widespread (Serrell and Raphling, 1992), recently there is an increased reliance on mobile devices such as smartphones and tablets, and particularly on the "Bring Your Own Device" (BYOD) model, where the museum offers digital content in form of mobile websites or apps and visitors can use their own devices to access it. In parallel, we see a corresponding shift in conceptualizing the role of interactivity as part of the visit: standalone kiosks represented specific moments or locations where digital technologies could enter the narrative of the exhibition, and were sometimes even confined to dedicated "media" or "IT" rooms. Nowadays, we commonly see digital narratives spreading throughout entire exhibitions or museums, often delivered through mobile digital content accompanying the visit.

The layering of physical and digital interactions and of analog and digital content is increasingly complex: for example, early mobile guides associated descriptive content to a specific exhibit (such as a painting in an arts museum), with separate analog content such as a physical label. Now we have digital or hybrid labels, a variety of digital content types to relate to the same exhibit (e.g., "fun" treasure hunts for children and families and in-depth analytical content for enthusiasts), and overall a more "transmedia" approach to interpretation with multiple interconnected narratives and modes of delivery (Kidd, 2014). Indeed, digital content and interactions are not just a substitute for more complex labeling, allowing for extended content, language choices or other forms of personalisation, but rather can create novel activities for visitors (beyond information delivery). Where early uses of digital technologies tended to centre on personalizing content delivery through themes, varying depth and style (with some exceptions, see e.g., *Future of Reading* exhibition; Harrison et al., 2001), it is now more common to see technologies enabling a range of activities: from playful engagement with museum topics, to individual "curation" through selection of favourite displays.

In the following, we focus our discussion of interaction frames first on how interaction relates to the museum environment and then on the form of augmentation. Other perspectives are possible: for instance, differentiating types of visitor activities, such as "taking a guided tour" and "doing a treasure hunt" or "playing a game". We will at times refer to activities, since these can be supported within different interaction frames and augmentation forms, as our focus here is on technologies used and their relation to the museum environment. We close with a discussion of attempts at providing links to post-visit interaction.

2.1   RELATIONSHIP TO THE MUSEUM ENVIRONMENT—SPACE AND VISITOR MOBILITY

We describe a first set of interaction frames that are distinguished by the relationship between digital interactive technologies and their physical incarnation with the overall museum environment, its spatial layout, and how it accommodates the physical mobility of visitors: standalone installations, mobile interactions, and assemblies. "Standalone" cases consist of one installation that is unrelated to other interactive elements that may be present, and set apart next to museum exhibits, but not directly interacting with the environment (i.e., the interaction is self-contained). Mobile interactions refer to cases when a visitor roams around usually carrying devices/technologies and the interactivity (which can be actively triggered by the visitor, or automatically "pushed" by the system) usually corresponds to locations or specific moments of a content narrative. With assemblies, the installation is made up of several components that are linked to each other and distributed across a site (this can include mobile technologies and standalone elements) in interconnected ways.

2.1.1   STANDALONE INSTALLATIONS

Standalone installations are deployed to create specific areas of an exhibition, or specific standalone exhibits, where digital interactions are a main feature. We mentioned the early examples of kiosks that were set up for the delivery of digital information. This format survives to this day, although with increasingly sophisticated devices, such as gesture and movement recognition systems. Possibly the most common form of standalone installations are information screens displaying illustrative content. Touch-screens have been widely employed for this purpose since the 1990s, however information screens can also be operated through simplified keyboards or trackballs.

Figure 2.1: Standalone installations are self-contained and either stand on their own, creating an "island" of interactivity within an exhibition area, or might be physically attached to the artefacts that they provide information about or otherwise relate to (illustration by Caroline Claisse).

A challenge when introducing such standalone interactive points is the overlay between digital content and physical displays, particularly linked to placement of kiosks. These can be placed in the vicinity of a particular exhibit or associated to "topical islands" within a gallery. Examples are the pods where interactive videos can be browsed, placed within the *Witness History* exhibition at the General Post Office in Dublin (Ireland), or the interactive screens at the Riverside Museum in Glasgow (UK). They are often placed in dedicated spaces, away from other exhibits, so as to encourage longer dwell-time and less distraction from artwork, but in some cases they are located within a gallery in support of a specific spatial narrative, although interaction with them is self-contained. Interactivity usually takes the form of browsing content or playing specific media such as videos or animations, but can also consist of problem-solving activities, simulation games (e.g., Kourakis and Pares, 2010), and other types of playful interaction aimed at engaging visitors with the exhibition themes.

The physical design of such installations is key in terms of supporting different interactions and different users. For example, in the early days of interactive screens, their small size meant often that they only allowed single-user experiences, with little room even for onlookers or peripheral participation. Height and ergonomics might affect which users can access kiosks, for example potentially excluding people with disabilities, and need to be carefully considered.

Figure 2.2: Different types of screen-based standalone installations. The small screens (left: Technical Museum Vienna, 2003) support individuals or at most pairs to interact, whereas the large multitouch table (centre: Museum of Natural History in Berlin, 2007) provides space for a crowd and onlookers. The Riverside Museum in Glasgow (right) uses a consistent design for information screens related to adjacent objects (photographs by Eva Hornecker, centre photograph from Hornecker, 2008).

In the evaluation of the *medien.welten* exhibition of the Technical Museum in Vienna (Hornecker and Stifter, 2006a), it was noted that information screens providing extensive information about the history of media, organised in a matrix across time and types of media, were used rarely. Logfiles revealed that most interaction sessions lasted only about 30 seconds, visitors tended to read only the first page of a series, and pages in the middle of the matrix were most frequently opened, indicating that visitors only checked out what type of content the screens offer. Interviews revealed that visitors did not want "to read this much information in the museum", and would have preferred information pertinent to objects in the direct vicinity. Displays that have a clearer relation to their environment fare much better, but they need to be carefully designed (see our later section Contextually embedded and Integrated).

Overall, the placement of standalone installations in a gallery is important in terms of exhibition design as it affects people's physical flow and groupings, and therefore how the interaction will unfold in relation to the displays and to other visitors. For example, in our early evaluation of the interactive points at the National Museum of Ireland at Collins Barracks (Ciolfi, Bannon, and Fernström, 2001), field observations showed how the placement of the kiosks affected how small groups of visitors distributed themselves in the galleries, often separating members in order for them to take turns using the installations. Another possible issue with placement is that the line of sight to relevant objects on display could be obscured by the positioning of the kiosk, making it less attractive for visitors to engage with the technology.

Evolution in technology means that standalone installations have taken up various physical forms—often making it easier to integrate the technology smoothly into the physical design of exhibitions. Technologies range from touchscreens (horizontal or vertical), image recognition, and other solutions, to traditional button and levers setups. Standalone installations can have any size, from a small table to comprising an entire wall.

The most defining feature remains that users must be in the installation's proximity and that interaction is confined to that point/location, without necessarily affecting the rest of the visit—unless the use of individual installations is part of a larger assembly of interactive encounters (as we will see in Section 2.1.3). Current approaches to interactivity via standalone installations can feature a varied and technically advanced range of input-output mechanisms, Examples are computer vision to recognise full body interaction in installations such as see *Lenses* and *Strike a Pose* at the ARTLENS Gallery, Cleveland Museum of Art.[1] Another example from the same museum is *Gaze Tracker*,[2] a large interactive display that reacts to the gaze of visitors via eye-tracking. While vertical touchscreens are predominantly used as information screens, these can also be used in more diverse ways. This form factor lends itself to content that is to be viewed on a vertical surface and where interaction is confined to lower areas of the display. Kourakis and Parés (2010) present a touchscreen wall created for a visitor centre for cave art in Spain. This depicts one of the post-paleolithic cave paintings from the nearby cave, which elements (animals, hunters) are brought to life via computer graphics animation and have autonomous behaviour. Importantly, the hunter figures can be controlled by touch gestures (making them run a short distance or shoot an arrow), while the animals react to the presence of hunters as well as to each other, up to a panicked stampede. This enables visitors (especially children) to experience first-hand, and experiment with and learn about hunting strategies and the teamwork required.

> **Interactive tables** started featuring in HCI research in museums and in commercial designs due to technological advances in the early 2000s. Interactive tables can physically accommodate more people and support concurrent interactions through multi-touch technology (Hinrichs and Carpendale, 2011). Not all interactive tables support multi-touch; some utilise other mechanisms, for instance buttons or tangible control elements.

A particularly successful form of standalone installations are interactive tables. It was hoped that tabletops would offer intuitive interaction through direct manipulation. Studies of how interactive tables are used and how interaction unfolds have shown that this interaction frame also needs careful design. Hornecker conducted one of the first studies of tabletop interaction in an

[1] https://www.museweb.wiki/gallery-one-the-lenses/.
[2] https://mw18.mwconf.org/glami/gaze-tracker/.

actual museum context: the *Tree of Life* installation at the Berlin Museum of Natural History (Hornecker, 2008). While visitors did not seem to be intimidated by the new technology, learning how to operate the installation required trial-and-error. But the conversations that people had around the table rarely focused on its content, and rather tended to discuss how to operate the installation itself. Several things besides usability issues contributed to this, including the content design and type of activity (browsing quiz questions), the perceived randomness of presentation, and lack of focus. Comparing a number of digital installations across the museum, visitors engaged more deeply with installations that offered limited, focused amounts of content while enabling visitors to choose and control how they investigated the content. This points to the importance of selecting suitable content and of supporting activities that visitors find valuable, that trigger and sustain conversation, and that contribute to meaningful and memorable experience, as discussed in Chapter 1.

In time, people's familiarity with this type of interaction and knowledge of how to design effective tabletop interactions have all increased. In their study of an interactive table at the Vancouver Aquarium, Hinrichs and Carpendale (2011) focused on the physical and social context of interaction. They noted that the gestures that users deployed to control the table's functionality also had an important role for personal expression, for example to communicate intentions to onlookers, subtly seeking mentoring from a companion, or would imitate what others had done. By virtue of their own physical set-up, tabletop interfaces afford a more performative kind of interaction than screen-based installations. Tabletop interaction has been deployed not only for information display but also for supporting informal education strategies, by scaffolding step-by-step sensemaking: Lyons et al. (2015) discuss the design of the educational game *Oztoc* at the New York Hall of Science. It is not intended for casual interaction, but is a structured activity teaching children about engineering practices and tinkering (Lyons et al. 2015). Studying how the installation supported the process, they found that it enabled children to quickly identify available resources, and also supported cooperative interaction between children and parents. Indeed, tabletop interaction in museums seems to have been most successful as part of educational exhibitions, for example about programming (Oh et al., 2013; Horn et al. 2014), biology (Loparev et al., 2016), or cultural history (Chu et al., 2015).

As the technology has become affordable, interactive tables have become very popular in museums as a means of enabling visitors to systematically browse historical data, frequently along a timeline that can be unfolded, or to engage in educational games related to the exhibition topic and to work with simulations. Tabletops (similarly to interactive wall displays) lend themselves to giving access to highly visual content that cannot be displayed as original item. The National Taiwan University, Microsoft Research Asia, and Taiwan's National Palace Museum (NPM) collaborated on a project to digitize and present fragile Chinese painting and calligraphy scrolls, resulting in four multi-touch tabletops (Hsie et al., 2013). These feature a multiresolution display, where those elements within a foveal area appear in a circular high-resolution looking-glass. Visitors can thus explore the art and further zoom into details, as well as drag the scroll left or right. Furthermore, an annotation icon gives access to the translation of calligraphy.

It should be noted that interactive tables do not need to be touch-sensitive. We have seen successful examples of different interaction mechanisms utilised: For example, the Robert Burns Birthplace Museum in Scotland, features a table with five large buttons around its rim. Up to five people (who can join at any time) can play against each other in a series of games where the timely pressing of buttons gives points. The table was very popular and often drew crowds, although some visitors would initially try to interact by touching the table, often taking quite some time to take notice of the buttons. A number of tabletop installations also include tangible tokens and manipulable elements that the interactive surface can detect, and which make the installation rather different in terms of how interaction occurs (especially among groups). We discuss these examples in Section 2.2.1, where we examine tangible and embodied forms of interacting with an installation.

2.1.2   MOBILE INTERACTIONS

Mobile interactive experiences have been one of the earliest forms of interactivity in museums. Analog audio guides have existed since the 1950s, and since the 1980s mobile digital devices have been adopted to deliver guidance to visitors or accompany them as they follow the narrative path of exhibitions in self-guided tours, as an alternative to guide-led group visit and as a way to suit an individual's pace and interests (Martin, 2000). Handheld devices provided by museums have evolved from basic digital audio players with headsets that deliver content through push-button interaction, to more complex and powerful computerised devices, which can deliver multimedia content or other digital services in correspondence to a particular location. Mobile interactions are still extremely popular as digital intervention in museums due to the widespread popularity of smartphones and tablets. Many museums (particularly smaller ones, with tighter budget and limited internal IT expertise) adopt a "Bring Your Own Device" approach, investing in the development of mobile applications and their content rather than a full-scale mobile hardware and software infrastructure with high maintenance costs. Personal devices include smartphones, tablets and increasingly also smart watches (Banerjee, Robert, and Horn, 2018).

Inextricably linked to mobile interaction is location detection. This can be enabled by various means: from proximity sensors (such as iBeacons), positioning systems (such as GPS), or by asking visitors to locate themselves by entering a location code or scanning an identifier such as a Quick Response (QR) code, to checking-in at particular points (via Near-Field Communication (NFC)).

Figure 2.3: Mobile digital devices such as smartphones can accompany visitors as they follow the narrative path of exhibitions in self-guided tours, offering digital content or interaction opportunities at different locations (illustration by Caroline Claisse).

QR codes (see Figure 2.4) are one of the most popular techniques, as they are cheap, do not require hardware infrastructure, and are easy to generate and manage (Atkinson, 2013). However, they are often criticised in terms of low aesthetic appeal, can be easily overlooked or ignored, either because visitors do not relate them with their experience (they can be interpreted to be for the use of staff), or because of their association with other services that are perceived as intrusive, such as advertising (Schulz, 2013; Wein, 2014). A recent approach to designing more effective and context-appropriate identifiers has been that of Artcodes,[3] where aesthetically pleasing patterns or meaningful images are used (Ali et al., 2018). In their study of Artcodes use at the Nottingham Lakeside Arts gallery (UK), Ali et al. also experimented with visitors designing their own Artcode markers and related auditory content, which was then exhibited in the gallery, and deemed highly engaging.

---

[3] https://www.artcodes.co.uk/.

Figure 2.4: Visitor scanning a QR code label via a mobile phone app. QR codes do not require hardware infrastructure, and are easy to generate and manage, and therefore can be an ideal solution for projects with low budgets or limited technical resources. They can be, however, aesthetically out of place (photograph by Luigina Ciolfi).

While the form of interaction itself is fairly standard (i.e., the visitor carries the device along and digital behaviour occurs at specific locations, either automatically or by active selection), the type of experience that mobile technology can support varies. Early examples were mainly for guiding purposes, often experimenting on the type of content to deliver (e.g., descriptive information vs. performative content, such as recitation or music), or on various themes underlying a visit (e.g., historical, biographical, artistic, etc.) that a user could select. Different styles of guiding can also be adopted, from displaying digital visual content such as floor plans for self-orientation, or directions to follow a predefined thematic visiting sequence. In the latter case, guidance is based on a narrative flow (i.e., connecting artefacts in a museum, or locations at a historic site), rather than on a map. But mobile technology is also used more and more to engage visitors in other activities and experiences, including more playful and open-ended activities, such as treasure hunts or creative tasks based on museum contents.

From its inception, mobile devices in museums have presented a number of challenges and potential problems. A frequently found issue is the social isolation that visitors can experience while using individual digital guides (particularly audio guides) (Economou and Meintani, 2011). Museum visits are profoundly social as they occur in public places and are most commonly undertaken with others. Social interaction is an essential part of the experience (Heath, vom Lehn, and Osborne, 2005), and when it is hindered or limited, the quality of the overall visit is negatively affected. A number of attempts have been made to overcome this: from changing the physical hardware to enable users to maintain an awareness of their environment and opportunities for social interaction (such as using single earpieces rather than headsets, or limiting the amount of audio in favour of visual content), to designing mobile experiences that are specifically intended for groups. An example of the latter is the *Sotto Voce* system, designed for the Filoli historic house in California with the intent of overcoming the social isolation "bubble" of audio guides (Aoki et al., 2002). Sotto Voce enabled visitors to eavesdrop on the content delivered to their companion, leading to discussions and conversations during the visit (Grinter et al., 2002). Another risk, particularly with multimedia guides, is that of distracting visitors from the heritage holdings surrounding them and focusing their attention onto the device's screen (vom Lehn and Heath, 2003; Filippini-Fantoni and Bowen, 2008; Othman, 2012; Petrelli et al., 2013).

As mobile guides evolved, elements of digital personalisation also emerged: enabling users to switch and adapt thematic paths, type or style of content, or via automated approaches to personalisation (e.g., the system monitors a user's behaviour and adapts its own behaviour). A body of HCI work exists on creating "smart" mobile experiences, adapting content to visitors' behaviour, or creating visitor profiles that determine how delivery of digital content is dynamically adapted (Not et al., 1998; Stock and Zancanaro, 2007). Given mobile interactive experiences tend to be designed for individuals, personalisation has been pursued through varying mechanisms: from adapting the delivery of content depending on previous choices and behaviour (based on algorithms, user models, and recommender systems), to giving visitors opportunities to actively create a personalised trail of the visit, for example by choosing pace, themes, or styles (Ardissono et al., 2011). Effects of personalisation can vary widely, depending on the mechanisms used: in some cases, the behaviour of the system can influence the behaviour of visitors rather than adapting to it. On the other hand, a visitor's awareness of the fact that the mobile interaction they are experiencing is different from that of companions can lead to discussion and debate, and to greater social interaction (Lanir et al., 2013).

Approaches to personalisation based on user modelling have been critiqued as they can render an already highly individual experience even more isolating, and tend to ignore contextual factors shaping the visitor's wishes and intentions as much as the cognitive characteristics of individuals (Not and Petrelli, 2018). Visitors within one group may have widely different preferences, and personalised tours that do not allow for pauses or common points might make it hard to have a shared experience. Museums often fear personalisation might not work as it often relies on overly simplified "types" of visitors (Serrell, 1997), and does not normally consider their motivations for visiting, in particular, how these can vary during the same visit (as identified by Ardissono, Kuflik, and Petrelli, (2011) and Not and Petrelli, (2018), in their extensive reviews of studies of personalisation for cultural heritage).

A number of mobile interactive experiences were created to go beyond descriptive information or guidance, and to experiment with more diverse ways to associate content and interaction to mobile interaction. The growth in approaches to gamification, where a visit is seen as an opportunity for (often educational) gameplay, means that mobile interactions have been designed as trails of discovery through shared tasks, such as solving open questions (Simarro-Cabrera et al., 2005), or collecting of items (such as locations, through "check-ins", or artefacts via photo-taking; O'Hara et al., 2007) and other activities, including tasks such as performing certain movements or using mobile devices as proxies for other objects such as swords, as in *The Lost Palace* installation by Historic Royal Palaces (Kidd, 2018a). "Treasure hunts" or "scavenger hunts" are popular forms of mobile activities: they are often intended for a younger audience, such as children and teenagers, however more generalist apps intended for a wider public often also contain a number of gameplay elements. Mobile quests and hunts also enable the collection of metadata such as tags, which can give the museum insights on visitors' understandings, preferences, and strategies (Cosley et al., 2009), and can integrate the use of social media for showcasing achievements, thus increasing the external visibility of the museum (Hillman et al., 2012; Weilenmann et al., 2013).

There is a risk with scavenger hunts and other similar gamified approaches to the visit that participants will only be concerned with the mechanics of the quest and concentrate on the competitive aspects, rather than on the heritage and linked narratives they relate to. For example, evaluation of the *Virtual Excavator* app for the Antonine Wall in Scotland (McGookin et al., 2012) showed that it did support greater memorability, but often also became the main focus of the visit as a game in itself, challenging visitors to quickly locate all the available content rather than reflecting on it. This is a trade-off to consider when introducing game-like mobile experiences, particularly if they are intended to have an educational purpose.[4]

Another example of mobile interaction frames is that of evocative trails, based on a mobile app where descriptive information delivery is not the priority in favour of more evocative content such as personal memories, fictional narratives, related artwork or music. Examples are the *Rock Art Mobile Project* (Galani et al., 2013), and the three mobile immersive experiences at UK museums described by Kidd (2018a): *Traces/Olion* at St. Fagan's National History Museum (part of

---

[4] Some museums have developed mobile gamified experiences with marketing purposes (for example, the Dallas Museum of Art; https://www.artsmanagement.net/index.php?module=News&func=display&sid=1762), or crowdfunding (National Museums Scotland; https://mw18.mwconf.org/glami/contactless-donations-experience/), where quests and hunts give visitors reward points toward special offers and discounts, or encourage them to donate to the museum in return for various benefits. These have proved very successful.

the National Museum of Wales), *I Swear To Tell the Truth* at the Imperial War Museum North in Manchester, and *The Lost Palace*, Palace of Whitehall (Historic Royal Palaces). These are described as forms of "artistic narrative interpretation" (Kidd, 2018a) based on characters that mix fact and fiction, adding an evocative and immersive layer to the visitor experience. Mobile evocative audio has also been used for unstewarded archaeological sites, such as the Antonine Wall in Scotland (McGookin et al., 2012). This mobile interactive experience adopted multimodal content to provide both some guidance for visitors to orient themselves in a rural site with little analog information available, and evocative ambient sounds intended to enliven the site.

Storytelling therefore becomes an important aspect of the design of this kind of mobile experience. The content that a museum has available thus needs to be complemented by creative approaches to storytelling. A similar approach was explored in the CHESS European Research project, where drama-based narrative techniques (stories about objects featured first-person narration by characters and were structured in episodes) were used to design a mobile experience at the Acropolis Museum in Athens, Greece. Evaluation of the prototype showed visitors particularly appreciating the humorous side of stories, and responding to them in humorous ways of their own, including smiling, nodding, and answering aloud (Roussou and Katifori, 2018). The results from this study also show that long narrative sections are not particularly favoured by visitors, in a similar way as with descriptive content. Challenges include the need to well develop the plot of a narrative to avoid being uninteresting or monotonous. Roussou and Katifori point out that to achieve this, cultural professionals need to abandon the "scientific voice" typically used in didactic visitor guidance, and thus lower the priority of scholarship and authenticity in favour of narrative flow. This can present a substantial challenge for museum staff responsible for interpretation.

Alternative content for mobile experiences can also take the form of prompts for visitor reactions and activities. Fosh et al. (2013) developed a "situationist" guide to the Rufford Abbey (UK) sculpture garden, designed following the principles of trajectory (Benford and Giannachi, 2011) where visitor engagement with the sculptures is supported by changing musical accompaniment and instructions for physical interactions to be performed in the vicinity of each sculpture. For example the sculpture *Young Girl* was accompanied by the song *Girl* by P.J. Harvey and the instructions: "*Why don't you take a closer look at this girl? Who is she? What does she look like?*" (Fosh et al., 2013, p. 151). The instructions for physical engagement with the sculptures added an element of performativity to the visit. The evaluation study shows that this often helped maintain stronger links and support coordination and sharing between the trajectories of co-visitors (pairs), but it made some participants self-conscious, with only a minority embracing all the opportunities to perform the most visible and flamboyant tasks.

Mobile interaction lends itself to guiding and supporting activities in open-air museums, and may enable technology support that would be impossible or costly to implement otherwise. We mentioned various examples from the literature (O'Hara et al., 2007; McGookin et al., 2012;

Galani et al., 2013; Fosh et al., 2013). The outdoor scenario posts both challenges and opportunities, for instance dealing with seasonality (McGookin et al., 2017; Weal et al., 2006) as the conditions of the site vary along with what visitors see and are able to do. Independent of the type of experience that mobile interactions support, general considerations to bear in mind when designing them regard crowding, ambient noise that might affect people's ability to hear auditory content, and existing support for wayfinding that might or might not support the mobile digital experience (Massung, 2012). Every museum or heritage site will need to be carefully studied so to plan mobile interactions in relation to the physical environment: for example, by avoiding the delivery of lengthy content in areas that tend to be crowded, thus affecting the physical flow of visitors. In the case of outdoor sites, seasonality is also a factor impacting the visitor experience that requires specific design decisions. Mobile interactive experiences might need to be tweaked in light of seasonal changes in natural lighting, landscape, climate, crowdedness, etc. that affect both the visitor motivations and intentions and the way the interactive experience is encountered (McGookin et al., 2017).

2.1.3   ASSEMBLIES

Assemblies of interconnected technologies and resources go beyond augmenting a specific room or object by embedding interactional threads across multiple spaces and exhibits. Whereas stand-alone installations work in isolation from other installations, assemblies work together as part of an overarching narrative or activity. When the interactive experience needs to be arranged in complex and pervasive narrative ways, or when themes are distributed over a large space and something is sought to create a connecting thread, such assemblages of multiple interactive and interconnected elements and platforms can be utilised. HCI is also increasingly concerned with interactions with and around distributed systems, where points of contact with digital interactive systems are part of an interconnected ecology of components, building up to a larger interactional narrative. Therefore, various examples of HCI research in museums have explored systems consisting of a heterogeneous set of devices and input/output mechanisms.

Assemblies can be simple, including only a few components, or more complex and layered. They can mix fixed screens and mobile elements, and also digital and analog elements. Analog or low-tech components can be a crucial part, as they can have the important function of linking different components, thanks to being wireless and without the need to be powered. "Assembly", as a concept in the context of exhibitions, was originally proposed by Fraser et al. (2003) and Bowers et al. (2007) as part of the SHAPE European project (Bannon et al., 2005). Assembly was not only defined as a type of interactive experience, but also as a "design scheme" centred around five principles. While these principles do not describe all possible assemblies, they do describe important common aspects common, most importantly the need for a coherent underlying narrative linking the various components.

According to Fraser et al. (2003), **designing an assembly** entails:

1. the definition of a unifying overall activity that people can engage in;

2. the design of an underlying information space that contains a variety of interrelated items, to be revealed as the activity progresses;

3. an assembly of interactive displays, with each display supporting a particular part of the common information space;

4. the use of common interaction techniques to promote the coherence of the experience across the different displays; and

5. a portable object/component with the role of accumulating a record of the visit and/or support identification as the visitors move around the space.

Figure 2.5: An assembly supports interconnected technologies across several spaces and object displays, and delivers an overall interactive narrative (illustration by Caroline Claisse).

Fraser et al. (2003) detail *The History Hunt*, an interactive visitor experience at Nottingham Castle (UK) developed through the Assembly framework. The History Hunt included a number of tangible and mixed-reality installations and low-tech paper artifacts. Guided by clues, visitors moved around the castle site collecting "locations" of remnants of the Medieval castle through a set of paper notes, which were tagged with RFID tags. The tagged paper could then be used to operate several installations that showed the castle site in different eras. The History Hunt supported participants in assembling knowledge about the castle, and progressively discovering and connecting locations and themes. Another example is the *Re-Tracing The Past* exhibition at the Hunt Museum in Limerick (Ireland) (Ferris et al., 2004) (see Figure 2.6). The exhibition theme was that of intriguing objects from the museum collection that could never be interpreted conclusively. Visitors could choose four objects, each represented by cards with embedded RFID tags. In one room of the exhibition, the card activated interactive stations where known information about each object was provided through various media (sound, dynamic projections, etc.). In the second room, the card was used to record visitors' own opinion about the objects. These audio files where made available to all visitors on a final installation: an interactive radio that could be used to browse all opinions, with each channel corresponding to one object. This is also an instance of visitor-generated content in an exhibition (see Chapter 3).

Evaluation of these two exhibitions showed the importance of low-tech portable objects (paper activity sheets and object cards) as lightweight connectors that both enabled interactions with the assembly and supported sense-making across the exhibition narrative (Fraser et al., 2004). Another key finding was that the higher the pervasive visibility of interaction (rather than being confined to a few interaction points), the greater the impact on other visitors and onlookers, particularly to encourage informal social interactions.

Reminisce at Bunratty Folk Park, an Irish open-air museum, is another example of assembly (Ciolfi and McLoughlin, 2017). The interactive experience explored everyday life in Ireland's past, and was deployed across several buildings. Visitors could collect, listen to, and respond to memories of the past as told by fictional characters. It comprised both mobile and standalone components: a mobile phone app for scanning, listening to, and recording memories; a set of evocative everyday objects that could be found at each house and collected as souvenirs, and that were used to operate a standalone installation in the Schoolhouse building, where other visitors' recordings could be heard. Evaluation echoed previous findings on interaction with assemblies, such as the role of low-tech portable artefacts (the souvenirs, as discussed in Ciolfi and McLoughlin, 2011), and the performative and socially engaging nature of interaction across various spaces at the same site. Findings show that the assembly mediated how visitors developed a sense of place attachment, by enabling them to link emotional and cognitive understanding to the various environments they explored. The tie to place was also strong in the physical design of installation components (for example, the use of everyday objects such as hanks of wool and pieces of turf as portable souvenirs), which resonated with the museum's aesthetic and tangible aspects. The nature of an assembly, whereby its components populate an exhibition or museum more pervasively than a standalone installation or a mobile experience, gives more opportunity to build on the environmental character of a site by means of tangible artefacts and meaningful materials, and it can for this reason be very effective in the context of historic sites.

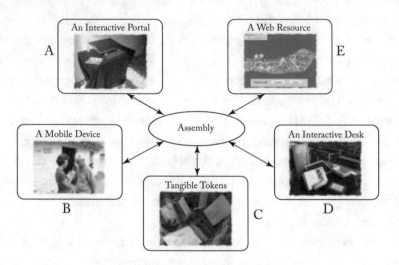

Figure 2.6: The *Reminisce* assembly: (A) the registration portal; (B) the mobile device (phone); (C) the tangible tokens; (D) the interactive desk; and (E) the web resource (image by Luigina Ciolfi).

An example of assembly for an indoor setting is the *Magic Worlds* exhibition at the Great North Museum: Hancock in Newcastle upon Tyne (UK) (Taylor et al., 2015). The exhibition engaged children in open, enquiry-based learning on the themes of folklore, myth, magic, and creativity. The interactive experiences consisted of three installations (two magic mirrors and a magic cauldron) that worked independently but were interconnected elements of an overall narrative. The exhibition had a trained Gallery Interpreter, who supported and orchestrated the experience. The installation was carefully placed to support the intended trajectory of discovery. Here, the physical design of the exhibition was of paramount importance, with the designers paying particular attention to creating a friendly, creative, and lively atmosphere that would encourage hands-on interaction. Taylor et al. (2015) discuss how the design of the installations supported the activities of the Gallery Interpreter, and conversely how the human "skilled storyteller" helped children and their families in progressive discovery of the exhibition.

A notable example of assembly in commercial exhibition design is the interactive experience at the Cooper Hewitt Smithsonian Design Museum in New York City. The museum went through a significant redesign, and a number of interactive installations (i.e., interactive table, interactive wall projections, etc.) were embedded at various points of the visit. The connecting theme and object tying it all together is the "Pen",[5] which not only enables visitors to interact with standalone installations, but also to collect artefacts, content, and locations across the museum to create a unique personalised trail of the visit that can also be found online (Dale, 2016). In this example, the portable, connecting element across the visit is also a means for continued engagement with the museum after the visit, tying on-site to online interaction. This fulfills some qualities of assemblies: the narrative is more fragmented, but it is an example of a commercial design that intentionally involves more than just mobile or standalone, and the portable component is a key to interaction at various points of the visit. The approach of enabling visitors to collect a digital trail of their activities and to access it later on was implemented earlier at different places, and some studies found that visitors only rarely access this digital trail (see, e.g., Hornecker and Stifter, 2006b).

Assemblies can work well for larger sites, and particularly historic sites, as they help overcome the risk of separating the point of interaction from the holdings on display. They provide opportunities for interaction linking multiple features of a heritage site, and via a variety of components that can create resonance with its tangible and material qualities. However, it is important to design assemblies that do not require visitors to engage with *every* component and do not impose a preordained sequence, as it can become prescriptive and too demanding, or would risk not delivering a "complete" narrative in case visitors skip a component or attend to them in a different order. Assemblies should allow for varied, fluid, and easily reconfigured forms of engagement and participation, particularly within small groups. Overall, however, assemblies and their design can be complex and time-consuming to create and manage, and ambitious in scale in terms of hardware and software as well as content and narrative. For these reasons, they might be unfeasible for smaller museums with limited digital expertise and limited external support.

2.2   THE RELATION TO THE FORM OF AUGMENTATION AND EXPERIENCE

As mentioned, the types of interactivity and interactions that different platforms can support are often interrelated, or can be combined and mixed. Furthermore, the relationship between interactive devices and the museum spaces and visitor mobility is not the only one aspect to be considered when examining possible interaction frames. In the second part of this chapter, we take a slightly different perspective on how we categorise interaction frames, which refers more to the type of interaction mediated, especially since a variety of platforms (mobile, standalone, etc.) can be involved in delivering an interactive experience.

In the following, we present three broad categories, based of how the digital technology relates to the form of augmentation and the form of experience that it affects.

---

[5] https://www.cooperhewitt.org/new-experience/designing-pen/.

- **Embedded and Embodied Interactions**: where interactivity is tightly interlinked with the material, tangible aspects of spaces and artefacts, and with embodied aspects of the visitor experience (Section 2.2.1).

- **Extended Reality**: where interactivity aims to achieve a seamless overlay of digital interactive content and behaviours on physical and analog spaces and objects (Section 2.2.2).

- **Multisensory Interactions**: where interactivity not only triggers audio or visual digital content delivery, but involves other sensory modalities (tactile, olfactory, etc.) (Section 2.2.3).

As mentioned, different technologies may be used across interaction frames, e.g., a body interaction interface may work as a stand-alone installation, or could be part of an assembly, or constitute an augmentation of original artefacts.

2.2.1   EMBEDDED AND EMBODIED INTERACTIONS

Embedded and embodied interactivity is tightly interlinked with the material, tangible aspects of spaces and artefacts, and with embodied aspects of the visitor experience. It is supported by augmented physical objects or physical spaces enabling tangible interactions (Hornecker and Buur 2006), and hands-on as well as full-body interactions.

Tangible interaction

> With **Tangible User Interfaces** (Ishii and Ullmer, 1997) and **Tangible Interaction** systems (Hornecker and Buur, 2006) the user interacts with a digital system by manipulating physical, tangible objects as interface elements. There is not just a generic mouse or abstract buttons, but instead a variety of diverse objects that enable rich physical interactions. These physical objects control the (digital) output of the overall system. Tangible Input in form of physical levers, handles, and wheels constitute some of the oldest forms of interaction within the museum context.

Interaction methods that can be categorised as tangible interaction are becoming increasingly common in museums. The introduction of tangible interaction elements changes how certain interactive frames operate and are experienced. For example, these can be part of a tabletop installations (discussed in Section 2.1.1) in form of purposely designed tangible tokens or everyday objects with embedded tags that users can manipulate and move about to control the interactivity. Shaer and Hornecker (2010) discuss the various strengths of tangible interfaces, several of which make them a good fit for the museum environment, i.e., supporting collaboration and awareness in groups, enabling "tangible thinking"' (thinking through bodily action), and direct (intuitive) inter-action. Studies in museums have confirmed and extended this.

Figure 2.7: In tangible interaction systems, visitors manipulate and move physical objects that are digitally interpreted. Frequently, tangible objects support interaction with interactive tables (left), enabling users to, e.g., place a query token on the surface to uncover information, and to move the resultant information bubble by moving the token. Some systems can detect the spatial arrangement of tangible objects, as in the example on the right where visitors playfully explore how the rough configuration of a church they create would be interpreted in different building styles (illustration by Katharina Bartholomäus).

Horn et al. (2009) compared the use of a tangible and a graphical interface to an exhibit that teaches about interactive computer programming in the Boston Museum of Science. The same visual programming language was presented on a screen allowing direct manipulation by mouse and with tangible puzzle-like elements that snap together in similar ways as the on-screen version. Around 260 museum visitors were observed and 13 family groups interviewed. It was found that children were more likely to approach the tangible programming exhibit, and also became more actively en-gaged with this. The effect appeared to be especially strong for girls. Ma et al. (2015) evaluated two versions of an exhibit that has visitors to the Exploratorium in San Francisco explore data on ocean microbes. Visitors investigate the distribution of four types of plankton by moving lenses across an ocean map showing an interactive visualization. In one version of the exhibit, the lenses are imple-mented as physical rings, in the other as virtual rings of the same size. While observations revealed no differences in demographics of visitors engaging with either version (unlike the study mentioned above), the tangible rings resulted in more interaction. Their physical affordances enabled touch and manipulation more than the virtual version, and thus encouraged initial interaction, which in turn was a precursor to continued engagement. It was also easier to explore larger areas of the map with the physical rings, whereas virtual rings had to be dragged across the table.

Everyday objects (usually with embedded ID tags) can also be used in conjunction with a tabletop or other "docking" installation, often to represent ideas, values, and perspectives that can present an exhibit in different light, or 3D replicas that allow visitors to experience what it is like to handle the artefacts. Physical objects enabling and controlling interactivity have also been used in forms that are pervasive across entire exhibits. Custom-built tangible objects or augmented replica objects may contain technological components and be networked with each other and other digital components in an exhibition (i.e., in Internet of Things interaction scenarios), such as the reactive everyday objects revealing alternative ideas and values described by Muntean et al. (2017). An example is *Flippin'* (Yoshino et al., 2017), a paper-based book interface for exploring a collection of sketches by Japanese artist Katsushika Hokusai (1760–1849). An 80-inch screen showing the sketches faces the book interface and reacts to manipulation of the book. Users interact by flipping the book's pages and touching a "touch-sign" for more information. The book has an introduction, a collection section, and a final quiz. Flippin' was installed in a public environment and evaluated in comparison with a touchscreen interface. Visitors were found to spend considerably more time with Flippin' than with the touchscreen, browsed more pages and pointed more often at images, in particular spending more time viewing the collection. The physical book-interface overall was most effective in raising and maintaining interest in the content, was easily understood, and enabled multi-user collaboration.

Figure 2.8: Visitors can playfully re-discover how Henri Tudor found out how to build a battery. They choose bottles with chemical fluids and insert battery plates into the battery casing in the middle of the table, which then reveals the movement of protons and electrons (top right). The left screen provides background information in response to which cards are placed on the blackboard (bottom right), the right screen reveals the battery capacity on graph paper (Maquil et al., 2017). © Luxembourg Institute of Science and Technology, 2019 (photographer: Christian Moll).

The form of custom-built objects can be chosen to resonate with a theme or location. Chu et al. (2016) envision digitally augmented portable tokens inspired by 16th century prayer-nuts as means to explore a narrative across various exhibits. This can also be done on a larger scale, where the entire exhibit consists of a manipulable configuration with tangible elements, or with collections of interacting objects. Maquil et al. (2017) built an exhibit resembling a scientists' workbench that enables playful discovery of the different steps and components required in building a battery for the Tudor Museum in Luxembourg (see Figure 2.8). Visitors can select components (electrolytes, plates, active paste) and insert them into a casing, activate the battery with a handle, and view results (electrolyte levels, growing layer size, moving electrons, capacity and estimated lifetime of the battery) on a simulated graph paper on a screen.

Such complex configurations with multiple elements are still rare. Nevertheless, many museum installations utilise elements of tangible interaction, having dedicated physical input controls (levers, wheels), that frequently emulate real-world devices (see Figure 2.9). For example, in the Riverside Transport Museum in Glasgow, visitors can enter a subway carriage, go into the drivers' cabin, and manipulate the gripper wheel to "steer" the audio-visual simulation of going through the tunnel and stopping at stations. At another installation, visitors push levers and turn wheels to load coal and water into a (simulated) steam train engine, and let off steam, thereby experiencing the difficulty of getting the train moving without overheating and the necessity for close collaboration of the engine team.

Figure 2.9: Tangible controls for large scale installations at the Riverside Transport Museum: visitors at the subway gripper wheel (left), at the lever and wheel controls of a steam engine (middle), and a parent taking the role of "banksman" to steer the ladder of a fire engine, with the child at the hose (photographs by Eva Hornecker).

Furthermore, physical objects carried by individual visitors can be used to control personalisation and record a unique "history" of the visit that can generate unique souvenirs or can be used by the museum for evaluation purposes. Pisetti, Not, and Petrelli (2018) describe two examples of this approach: at an outdoor heritage site (First World War trenches in the Italian Alps), thematic cards were carried around by visitors and used to trigger auditory content at various locations when placed inside a pouch on a belt worn by a visitor; at an indoor exhibition at the Museum of War in Rovereto (Italy), a portable interactive object operated hybrid displays and generated a personalised postcard as memento and to access additional content online. This role may also be taken by augmented replicas that mimic authentic museum objects (Roozenburg, 2013). *The Hague and The Atlantic Wall* exhibition held at MUSEON (The Netherlands) (Marshall et al., 2016) told the story of how the German-occupied city was affected by the construction of the Atlantic Wall defence fortifications in World War II. Replicas of historical artefacts (such as a German beer mug and a pack of sugar substitute) represented unique personal (Dutch or German) perspectives on historical facts, and could trigger digital content at various points of the exhibition. The original objects were also on display. Evaluation shows that visitors selected objects not on the basis of physical qualities, but rather for the perspective represented, with the Dutch civilian being the most popular (Marshall et al., 2016). A comparative study of visitors' preferences of how to deliver the same content: a mobile phone app, smart cards, and the smart replicas found that tangible means of interaction (cards and replicas) were favoured by visitors of all ages over the app (Petrelli and O'Brien, 2018).

While interactions featuring tangible objects have in general been successful, their design needs to take into account some possible risks: one is the limited lifespan of objects that are manipulated by numerous visitors and can become damaged or wear out, requiring regular replacement, which can add to workload and cost of an exhibition. Another issue is that, unless the installation clearly emulates a real-world interaction, visitors who may be used to mobile apps and touch screens may find these more obscure at first. In this respect, design of signage and accompanying materials is key to direct visitors, particularly at times when an exhibition is quiet and there are no other people to observe using the technology and to emulate.

Tangible interactions can also be more broadly embedded into spaces. The *Kurio* museum guide (Wakkary et al., 2009) comprised a tabletop installation, a personal digital assistant, and a set of three portable tangible interaction controllers (a *listener*, *pointer*, and *reader*). The guide was intended for small family groups in playful support of their visit through game learning. Evaluation shows that participants appreciated how the tangible components could be manipulated and shared, and that they were seen as active, fun, and intriguing. However, users also felt it took some time to learn how all components worked—individually and together, and in relation with the exhibition space (Wakkary et al., 2009).

Contextually Embedded and Integrated

Interactive exhibits (high- or low-tech) often fail their purpose because they lack an effective spatial and conceptual relationship with the exhibited artefacts (Pujol-Tost, 2011), distracting or isolating from the context. Pujol-Tost suggests that technology should be integrated and intertwined with the museum space and its artefacts. Following this thought, Hornecker defines interactives that are highly integrated with the museum environment and surrounding artefacts as *contextually embedded* (Hornecker, 2016). In terms of our prior classification in Section 2.1, these can be categorised as midway between standalone and assemblies. They augment the existing objects and environment, but do not have the scale of an assembly.

Digital content is provided in a way that directs attention *toward* the exhibits and engages visitors with these. Often, this content only conveys its full meaning in this context.

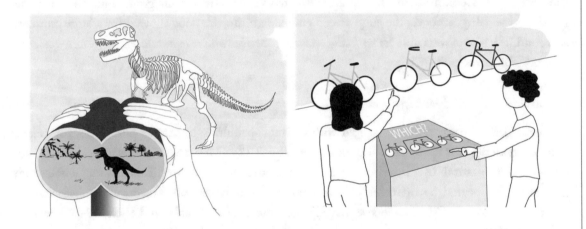

Figure 2.10: Contextually embedded installations directly relate and refer to surrounding exhibits, and invite or even require visitors to engage with these, as when visitors are to select the correct bicycle as answer to a quiz question (illustration by Katharina Bartholomäus).

The relationship with the heritage holdings and the physical environment is important in these cases, as Hornecker details for the *Jurascopes* at the National Museum of Natural History in Berlin (Germany): periscope-like devices placed at two locations in the outer corners of the dinosaur hall where all skeletons can be seen. When pointed at a specific skeleton, the Jurascope will display digital 3D animations showing the live animal in its natural environment, in an informative and entertaining short scene (Hornecker, 2010). A large screen is also embedded at an angle into the floor on the right-hand side of each set of Jurascopes, intended for visitors for which the Jurascopes are not accessible, such as wheelchair users and children. Here, skeletons are selected by turning a large lever next to the screen (Hornecker, 2016). While the installation is not highly interactive, its placement in the context and orientation toward the skeletons in the hall is crucial. Visitors easily and quickly relate information from the animated scenes to the skeletons, looking and pointing back and forth. This fosters conversation and group sense making, thus contributing to learning processes.

Contextually embedded installations invite visitors to draw connections between the content provided by a digital installation and surrounding exhibits. Enabling factors of design (Hornecker, 2016) include clear lines of sight (being able to glance from the digital content over to the real object), visual salience (it being easy to see and recognise key elements, to, for example, determine which item on the screen corresponds to physical artefacts in the space around it), users being in control (having time to think and discover connections, and to talk about them), and support for sharing (connections being visible to bystanders so as to allow for shared understanding). With the Jurascopes, the screen version was far more successful in supporting shared experience than the periscopes. Looking through the latter isolated viewers from their group, and did not allow for shared viewing, whereas the large screen embedded into the floor allowed for a large crowd to surround it. Visitors were able "*to mutually orient to the screen and to communicate, negotiate, and enjoy themselves*" (Hornecker, 2016).

Embodied and Bodily interaction

Spaces and artefacts can be augmented with digital capabilities, but the opportunities for greater bodily interaction for visitors are also increasing. The 2012 NMC report (Johnson et al., 2012) anticipated that "natural" user interfaces will soon be common in museums. This includes whole-body interaction supported by off-the-shelf platforms (such as Microsoft Kinect) and newer sensing technologies. Most of the immersive installations described by Snibbe and Raffle (2009) also fall into this category.

> In **embodied or bodily interaction**, visitors' bodies are tracked and recognized, their posture or movement constituting the "input" that a system reacts to. The reactive space may be wall- or floor-based. Visitors may interact with or uncover existing media and contents or generate new content.

While here we focus on whole-body interaction, gestural interaction has also become more prominent in museums, where users' hands and arms may be tracked to control an application. A famous early installation is the *Virtual Conductor* installed in 2000 in Vienna's House of Music Museum:[6] here visitors pick up an infrared baton and the orchestra seen on screen (in multi-track videos that can be pitch-shifted) responds to the gestures made, translated to speed, volume, and instrument emphasis. With new technologies, it has become possible to directly track gestures. Chen

---

[6] https://hci.rwth-aachen.de/po, http://eguide.hdm.at/hdm/objects/the-virtual-conductor/28/.

et al. (2011) developed an application that detects visitors' finger movement within a semi-closed black box to control Chinese shadow puppetry animations.

Figure 2.11: Whole-body interaction comprise interactive installations that react to visitors' movement (right), but may also rely on other forms of including visitors' bodily behaviour as part of sense-making and engaging with content (left) (illustration by Katharina Bartholomäus).

Bodily interaction increases engagement and can support social interaction, thereby potentially fostering learning. Snibbe and Raffle (2009) provide seven design principles for immersive, body-based installations in the museum context. These include having the user experience the media in a visceral way, emotionally and physically via whole-body interaction, before entering a more symbolic or rational phase; that the media needs to be immediately and predictably responsive; to allow for variability; and to allow for scalable interactions—that is, interaction becomes richer as more people are involved.

Whole-body interaction is immersive by definition—the user becomes the interface, experiences the media in a visceral (physical and emotional) way, and the installation reacts directly. An example is *Strike a Pose* at the ARTLENS Gallery, Cleveland Museum of Art, where visitors are asked to replicate the full-body posture of a statue and given feedback on how accurately they have matched it (Alexander et al., 2017). Beside being a playful way to engage with artwork, the installation also conveys that sculptures are not always static representations but can also capture moments as part of complex movements, and enables visitors to experience the expression or emotion that a posture conveys (Steier, 2014; Alexander et al., 2017). Art can thus be experienced via proprioception, eliciting empathetic feelings and emotions (Bacci and Pavani, 2014). Steier (2014) analyzes how posing as an embodied, gestural activity contributes to visitors' meaning-making in understanding and interpreting paintings. He observed visitors encouraged to recreate Edvard

Munch's self-portraits by posing and taking pictures in the National Museum of Art in Oslo. Notably, visitors often also began to mimic figures of a painting on their own accord.

There has also been research on how whole-body interaction can foster understanding of abstract concepts (Malinverni and Pares, 2014). Theories of embodied cognition suggest that this might be beneficial in terms of memorability and informal learning, and suggest direct connections between gesture and thought as well as learning. Physical actions may be used to transmit and convey meaning, or abstract concepts may be conveyed via embodied metaphors, for instance by illustrating the concept of "balance of social justice" by balancing one's bodies. However, there are still open questions as to when bodily immersion benefits learning or might actually discourage reflection. While some studies comparing traditional interfaces and whole-body interfaces found the former to be more effective for learning, others found the opposite (Malinverni and Pares, 2014). Dancstep et al. (2015) compared visitors' activities and experiences at immersive and tabletop exhibits with the same content (geometry) in the San Francisco Exploratorium. In the whole-body version, the system draws voronoi diagrams around users' bodies on the floor, whereas for the tabletop version, users move pegs on a board and the system overlays voronoi diagram lines. The only difference is thus that, in the immersive version, the visitor "is the peg'" and inside the diagram. Interviews and observations suggest that while the immersive version resulted in more repeat visits and was more fun and engaging, learners at the tabletop exhibit engaged in more content-related discourse and reasoning. A similar comparison was conducted by Roberts and Lyons (2017) as experimental study in a museum. They varied means of control (whole-body vs. a handheld tablet controller) as well as single- vs. multi-user input for an exhibition on the visualisation of census data. Findings indicate that the handheld controller, in particular in the single-user condition, produced the most learning-relevant talk.

An underlying reason for why whole-body interaction does not fare as well as hoped may be that immersive exhibits make it harder for visitors to move between diving in (immerse themselves and be active) and out (reflect and analyse) (Ackermann, 1996), as it is inherently harder to get a "bird's eye perspective". Whole-body interaction might therefore be more appropriate in contexts that benefit from immersion, for example, when the goal is to trigger emotions and to empathise, or when physical interaction enables development of tacit understanding of concepts that are directly and clearly mapped to the physical interaction.

2.2.2   EXTENDED REALITY

With "extended reality" we refer to technologies that overlay digital content and behaviours mapped onto tangible and analog spaces and objects: namely, Virtual (VR), Augmented (AR), and Mixed Reality (MR). While VR refers to a fully artificial, computer-generated environment, usually presented as a 3D audiovisual, AR overlays computer-generated information over a real environment in real time: in this case the real environment can still be perceived underneath the augmentation. In MR, real and virtual elements are merged in one world and can interact, i.e., interaction with virtual elements influence real-world components. Furthermore, we briefly discuss projected AR (also known as projection mapping, or spatial augmented reality). Bekele et al. (2018) provide a detailed survey of the state of the art in how AR, MR and VR have been utilised within cultural heritage, and describe technologies used for tracking and augmentation as well as for interaction. Moreover, they differentiate different uses of the technology (for learning, often about history), for enhancement of exhibitions, for exploration, (virtual) reconstruction, and for virtual museums.

Virtual Reality

Due to its immersivity, VR is often used to propose reconstructions of environments or to enable visitors to experience historical scenes/episodes from a first-person perspective. As users need to either wear a headset (head-mounted displays or VR goggles) or enter a specially designed space with large-scale projections (while usually wearing VR goggles for 3D vision) to achieve immersivity into an artificial digital environment, the use of VR in museums and galleries has always been the subject of intense debate: it requires costly technology and resources, and can be an isolating experience that occurs away from heritage spaces and objects; on the other hand, it can deliver powerful immersive experiences, conveying rich information (Gillam, 2017). Generally speaking, VR is considered well-suited for standalone immersive experiences in dedicated rooms or for virtual museums, and ill-suited for exhibition enhancement (Bekele et al., 2018).

> **Virtual Reality** is the experience of a computer-generated, 3D virtual world. Users can navigate in 3D, at minimum via head movement. The virtual world can be visual and/or auditory. For 3D stereoscopic vision, users need to wear specific glasses or headsets. VR can also offer the possibility for interaction (as well as viewing a scene), via movement and manipulation of objects. Early experiments with VR in museums relied on "VR theatre" settings, where visitors donned VR goggles to watch a 3D movie in a cinema room. Contemporary approaches enable a more active experience.

There have been experiments with VR applied to cultural heritage for many years, to fully immerse visitors in recreations of historical sites, often with the goal of contextualising museum artefacts, or to enable close-up exploration of objects (Tsichritzis and Gibbs, 1991; Roussou, 2000). Commonly used metaphors for VR installations are those of travel (e.g., traveling through time and/or witnessing a historical event or place), character impersonation (e.g., the visitor takes on the identity of a character and sees a world/situation through their eyes), or reveal (e.g., the visitor can see a hidden layer of the place they are in) and reconstruction (e.g., seeing what a ruined castle looked like). For example, the *Keys To Rome* project (www.keys2rome.eu) developed VR exhibitions with gameplay elements that were exhibited in dedicated spaces at four heritage sites connected through the theme of Roman culture: the Trajan Market in Rome, City Hall Vijecnica in Sarajevo, Allard Pierson Museum in Amsterdam, and the New Library in Alexandria (Egypt), that could be explored through the "eyes" of a character from Ancient Rome (Pescarin, 2014).

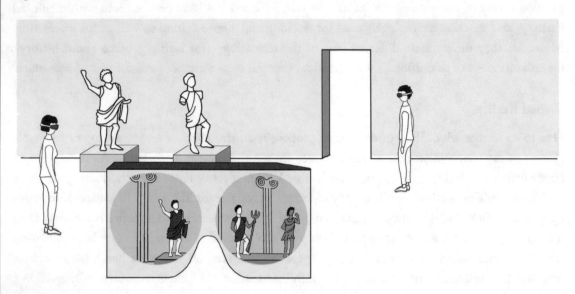

Figure 2.12: VR provides an alternative view replacing the real world. While usually VR is used to create fully artificial worlds, in museums it is often used to recreate the past, showing museum artefacts in their original state and context and to bring them to life. Here the statues are shown as they used to stand on a frieze in their original environment. Visitors can explore them by navigating in physical, 3D space. (Note that wearing VR goggles as in the image occludes the view of the real world—our visitors here thus would actually risk bumping into each other!) [Illustration by Katharina Bartholomäus.]

Virtual Reality can be experienced within the museum or can enable a "virtual visit". The *Google Arts and Culture* project collaborated with the Berlin Museum of Natural History and the London Natural History Museum to allow virtual visits, based on indoor StreetView.[7] The experience becomes immersive when users wear a cheap headset (Google cardboard), and see additional digital content such as ancient species coming back to life (Bryan, 2016). The Städel Museum in Frankfurt, Germany, created an app that enables users wearing a headset to move through the museum as it looked in 1878, when it opened (Jürgs, 2017).

VR has been used for ancillary activities to museum visits, such as (pedagogical) exploration games (Champion, 2015) and ambient games (such as in the REVEAL project[8]), which can take

[7] http://www.nhm.ac.uk/press-office/press-releases/museum-and-google-launch-google-arts---culture-natural-history-.html.

[8] http://revealvr.eu/2018/09/17/the-chantry-launched-on-european-playstation-store/.

place online or at other sites such as schools, as follow-up to a physical museum visit. The Digital Humanities field also championed the use of 3D reconstructions and VR environments for preservation of heritage objects and places (as well as for interpretation), also as alternative to enable some form of heritage visit for audiences who cannot or do not want to travel (Champion, 2011).

Contemporary artists are also making use of VR in their work, which is intended to be experienced through VR by visitors to a gallery. For example, director and designer Zach Richter created an immersive VR visual and musical performance of Leonard Cohen's popular song *Hallelujah*, combining 3D visuals and 3D audio. The performance takes place all around the viewer, who wears a head-mounted display and can explore the virtual scene (visually and acoustically) at 360° by moving around a specific space. The piece was exhibited at The Musée d'Art Contemporain (MAC) in Montréal (Canada[9]) as part of their flagship exhibition on Leonard Cohen,[10] in a dedicated area separate from other exhibits and accessible by one visitor at a time.

Overall, it is very challenging to integrate VR into museums. The setup if often (and unavoidably) confined to separate spaces, where the connection with exhibits might not be clear. Experiences are often limited to small groups or lone individuals, and cannot be shared, particularly when making use of wearable displays. VR in museums furthermore suffers all known issues of VR, including that a proportion of people experiences simulator sickness from inconsistencies between visual perception and self-motion or inconsistent depth cues. Early experiments with VR in museums also suffered from the quality of 3D imagery. However, VR is becoming more aesthetically pleasing and fitting for heritage environments. Furthermore, cheaper and more accessible platforms such as Google Cardboard are available (as well as higher-end, but still low-cost platforms such as Oculus Rift, Microsoft HoloLens, and the HTC Vive), resulting in a rising number of projects and apps such as described by Jürgs (2017).

Pujol-Tost and Economou (2007), in an evaluation of VR in exhibition settings, note how exhibitions and VR correspond to two completely different models of communication: one where the content is laid out in full and visitors can explore it (together or apart) in their own time and own pace, and a highly constrained and often lonely experience that is navigated according to tight boundaries. They question whether VR and exhibition design can work in synergy at heritage sites, and suggest that perhaps VR is better suited for companion experiences. Gillam (2017) also notes that technical glitches combined with inadequate storytelling efforts via a medium that is deeply different from more established interpretation platforms in museums can cause problems and discourage visitors from engaging (Gillam, 2017). Overall, however, VR has been one of the most problematic technologies to bring into heritage settings in terms of cost, physical and technical setup, and obsolescence. Nonetheless, VR technology is rapidly progressing and this includes the possibility of including other people into a VR space as realistic 3D avatars, which could interact

[9] https://macm.org/en/exhibitions/leonard-cohen/.
[10] http://www.zacharyrichter.com/hallelujah/.

amongst themselves and with "physical" visitors. While it is likely that the technology will take some time before becoming mature, manageable, and affordable in museum settings, it might lead to novel and more social experiences of VR.

Augmented Reality (Mobile or Nonmobile)

For several reasons, AR has been for some time a promising avenue: as it anchors and overlays digital content (usually visually) onto physical environments, while maintaining view and perceived presence of the actual environment, it has been identified as more suitable (than VR) to provide digital interactive content in exhibition settings and to better integrate into them (Schavemaker et al., 2011; Elinich, 2014; Bekele et al., 2018). Mobile AR has proven particularly successful, also in conjunction with the popularity of BYOD ("Bring Your Own Device") approaches as part of museums' digital strategies. Furthermore, smartphones and tablets have become powerful enough to enable good quality AR experiences. Other platforms have been explored, such as Google Glasses, however they pose problems: they are not as robust, they are uncomfortable to wear, and do not support the granularity of control required in museums when focusing on smaller objects or closely laid-out exhibits (Mason, 2016).

> **Augmented Reality** overlays and spatially aligns computer-generated virtual elements onto a view of the real world, adding virtual elements or masking parts of the real view. Unlike VR, AR only alters the view of the real world and does not replace it. Similarly, augmentation may use other modalities besides vision. AR may be presented via dedicated goggles (similar to VR), but it has become common to use mobile devices with integrated video cameras which enable exploration of the environment with mobile or "handheld AR".

AR is used commonly as interpretation aid at sites where embedding technology into the environment would be difficult, jarring, or unfeasible; e.g., living history museums, archaeological sites, historical buildings. The common aim is similar to VR: overlaying digital content to show aspects of the heritage site/artefacts that cannot be viewed easily by other means. For example, some AR applications show reconstructed ancient buildings, or views from past historical periods. Early research applications to museums include the ARCHEOGUIDE (Vlahakis et al., 2004) and LIFEPLUS (Sforza et al., 2001) projects, which experimented with mapping 3D content onto physical spaces on notebook computers (with integrated cameras and orientation sensors). In their evaluation of an early AR guide at the Museum of Fine Arts in Rennes (France), Damala et al. (2008) found a clear split in participants' opinions regarding whether the system helped them appreciate the artworks or distracted them. The participants were also conscious of being alone in the evaluation trial, while they would normally visit museums with other people, therefore expressing concerns regarding how the technology would affect the social dimension of the visit. These find-ings, and those of more recent evaluations of AR-interactive experiences for museums, echo those relating to other immersive technologies and their potential to isolate people, independently of the added value that these installations can provide.

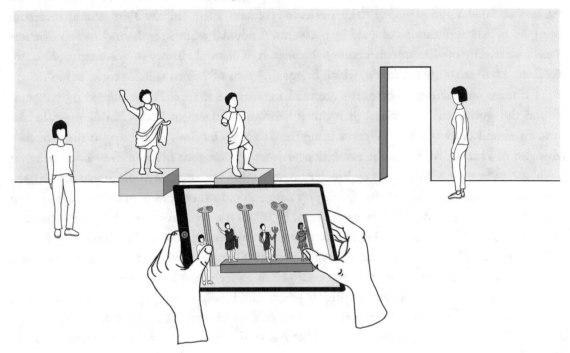

Figure 2.13: AR overlays and aligns virtual elements onto a view of the real world. Visitors can explore their surrounding for the AR overlay information. Here, colourings and missing parts of the statues and some elements of the original surround context are added on top of a video view captured by the mobile device (illustration by Katharina Bartholomäus).

Other early educational AR applications developed at the HITLab in New Zealand exper-imented with controllers to trigger interactivity in science centres, museums, and exhibition halls. Examples included handheld visors/looking glasses in combination with marker-based AR, where the augmentation is overlaid onto markers (computer-vision recognised images), and users interact, for example, by turning the pages of an interactive storybook (Woods et al., 2004). This way of interaction is referred to as "tangible augmented reality". Evaluation of prototypes showed that AR was effective in conveying spatial and temporal concepts to users, but that users needed guidance to understand an interaction frame that was completely novel to them (i.e., holding the visor correctly, understanding that each marker corresponded to a 3D object).

Nowadays, (mobile) AR is a consolidated platform, used by large gaming communities (such as in the case of PokémonGo). AR guides and visiting companions have become widely popular at museums across the world. The quality and pleasantness of 3D content has hugely improved, and so have the technical capabilities to accurately identify "target" objects or locations (without dedicated markers or labels) and promptly deliver relevant content. There are countless current successful examples of AR applications adopted by museums. A popular example is the mobile app *Skin and Bones*[11] offered by the Smithsonian National Museum of Natural History in Washington, D.C. for its "Bone Hall" anatomy exhibition, which brings skeletons of various animals back "to life".

Similar interaction mechanisms are used for many AR applications offered by museums around the world, and by national or regional heritage management bodies, for example, in historic cities and outdoor sites.[12] Visitors using the *Stitching Our Struggle* AR app at the Canadian Museum of Human Rights in the exhibition *Freedom of Expression in Latin America* could hover a tablet device over a patchwork embroidery representing the story of Chilean activist Carmen Quintana to "pull" the object from the display case and onto their screen, examine it closely and then access additional digital content (Gillam, 2017). Some applications of AR have a stronger focus on informal learning. *Spark* is an augmented exhibit on circuitry at The Museum of Science and Industry in Chicago; it includes a tangible circuit building environment and a simulator where a tablet serves as AR-view lens onto the built circuit to see a simulation (Beheshti et al., 2017). *Spark* was experimentally evaluated with 60 parent-child pairs comparing the AR setup with a single display one. Results show that the children performed better in a post-test activity in their understanding of circuit building after using the AR version. Furthermore, the AR version enabled greater communication between parent and child as well as resulting in different distribution of roles, the parent tending to act less as instructor and more as a co-learner (Beheshti et al., 2017).

The core of interaction with AR remains the exploration of content across a physical exhibition or heritage space, by positioning a viewing device so to detect specific targets. However, in some examples, interaction with the mobile device involves more than just triggering content delivery, and can include "collecting" items and locations, and thus giving a different agency. For example, the exhibition *Story of the Forest*[13] at the National Museum of Singapore enabled visitors to not only view digital content through an AR app, but also to collect digital plants and flowers "scattered" throughout the space. Other applications include, for example, the creation of AR artworks for contemporary galleries, where the digital layer is not just an add-on, but a work of art in itself (Geroimenko, 2018). An example is an exhibition of work by AR artists held in 2016 at Boston Cyberarts[14] gallery (Boston, MA).

---

[11] https://naturalhistory.si.edu/exhibits/bone-hall/.
[12] http://www.heritagecities.com/stories/explore.
[13] https://www.nationalmuseum.sg/our-exhibitions/exhibition-list/story-of-the-forest.
[14] https://bostoncyberarts.org/art-augmented-reality/.

While the application of AR in museums has dealt predominantly with visual content, there have been some explorations of prototypes for haptic AR experiences, so to simulate touching a 3D digital object (Dima, Hurcombe, and Wright, 2014). These, however, arc not yet available to the general public and remain the object of current research. It is worth noting that auditory augmentation also fits under the definition of AR, and thus, interpreted strictly, an audio guide with reactive, localised audio is a form of AR.

AR brings a new set of challenges for usability and user experience. Hunsucker et al. (2018) found that for usability testing of AR museum experiences (using the HoloLens) it was important to test in the real setting, since this would provide insight into how users interact with the spatial setup, e.g., how they walk around and explore both the real exhibits (statues) on display and the virtual statues displayed next to them. It was vital to test the spatial arrangement of AR content with real artefacts and the effect this had on navigation pathways and visual orientation of visitors, including that of other visitors in the same space. Placing virtual elements into empty spaces could block pathways or result in other visitors disrupting someone's experience by walking through the virtual objects.

Other issues crucial to the success of AR installations are robust infrastructure and connectivity to enable smooth and prompt display of content in response to interactions, appropriate storytelling that suits the medium, and consideration for the contextual condition of use, such as lighting and crowdedness (Schavemaker et al., 2011; Roussou et al., 2015). As mobile AR often operates on devices of relatively small size, issues of social isolation have been tackled by, for example, displaying part of the digital content and a representation of the interactivity on public screens visible to onlookers (Madsen and Madsen, 2016).

Projected AR (or Spatial Augmented Reality)

> **Projected AR** is a special case of AR that does not require viewers to carry dedicated equipment. Instead, projectors are installed to project visual augmentations onto the object in question. The projection thus needs to "work with" the physical surfaces available. Sophisticated methods accurately wrap projections onto a surface, so they appear realistic. This is called projection mapping, video-mapping, 3D-projection, or spatially augmented reality. The approach is best known from façade mapping, often used at urban festivals. Projection requires dimly lit environments in order to produce the intended visual effects and thus is not always feasible. As it can suffer from occlusion by other objects (that cast shadows), projectors are usually installed at an elevated position.

Projected AR avoids visitor isolation, enables group experience (since everyone sees the same view), and requires no mobile equipment (Ridel et al., 2014). Famous early examples include the *Singing Heads* in Disneyland's Haunted House (1969) (cf. Mine, 2012). Projection mapping can create impressive optical spectacles and illusions, not only using the existing object as a surface, but making it move, warping it, breaking it up, or changing its materiality (for example overlaying a different visual texture such as wood over a metal object, etc.). Done well, it can create the experience of a presence that is hard to achieve with purely virtual content. Projected AR (just like standard AR) in itself is not interactive, but can be made reactive or interactive. Most projection mapping to date is non-interactive, but some projects enable visitors to explore objects: for instance, using the metaphor of a flashlight that reveals details of the original object that weren't visible before, or using one's finger to point and reveal visual augmentations (Ridel et al., 2014).

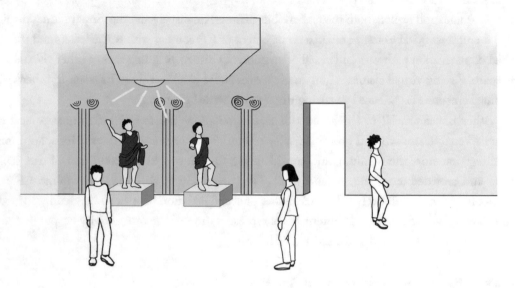

Figure 2.14: Projected AR is projected directly onto the physical world, mapping the visuals with the environment. For this to align properly, the geometry of the real environment needs to be taken into account, so that for instance, the colouring of the statues does not bleed onto the wall (illustration by Katharina Bartholomäus).

Halskov and Dalsgaard (2011) used 3D-projection onto a large statue to communicate the myths about *Holger the Dane*, using elements of storytelling, atmosphere, and integrated sound. The projection reacts to visitors' approaching to bring the statue to life, making its eyes glow, and soon, a fairy flies around the statue, lending Holger power by sprinkling fairy dust. The statue also seems to breathe, when later falling asleep.

Recently, a number of projects have provided museum visitors with an illustration of what Egyptian or Greek stone engravings looked like (colouring them in by using non-destructive means), directly projecting on the historical artefacts: examples are mapped projections on the side wall of the Temple of Dendur at the Metropolitan Museum of Art in New York showing how it was originally painted.[15] Besides of recreating colour, the projection can also highlight and enlarge the hieroglyphs and animate the "flat" drawings to explain how these represent 3D scenes. Another example is the Aztec Coyolxauhqui Monolith, a large circular monolith over 3 m wide in diameter (11 ft) and carved in low relief, found on site and currently exhibited at the Museum of the Templo Mayor in Mexico City (see Figure 2.15). The entire gallery was redesigned to enable visitors to view the stone from above, at a distance sufficient to see its whole surface, upon which a cyclical set of mapped projections shows its original colours and how they relate to each other according to ancient religious symbolism.

Torpus (2018) discusses the design and experiences with a number of installations that use 3D projection to, e.g., provide x-ray views to explain the functioning of Roman wall and floor heating systems on an archeological site, and animated stains on the bedsheets of a Swiss farmhouse evoking a sick-bed scene. A core design principle was to contextually extend the existing site using hidden technology. Evaluation revealed that the projections were appreciated by visitors and museum professionals. They enabled visitors to keep their locus of attention and enhanced emotional involvement. Careful interaction design, in particular regarding timing (of reactions as well as duration) was important.

Figure 2.15: Projection mapping onto the Coyolxauhqui Monolith (Museum of the Templo Mayor, Mexico City), progressively revealing its original colours and shading (photographs by Luigina Ciolfi).

Mixed Reality

A more complex model (in terms of interaction and technical and physical set-up) of deploying digital technologies to extend reality is MR. It is characterised by interconnection between physical and digital points of interaction, and overlay of action and effect in the physical and virtual world, where digital (often 3D) and physical spaces and objects coexist in real time. Collaboration support is a

---

[15] https://www.metmuseum.org/blogs/digital-underground/2015/color-the-temple provides a detailed report on the research and development process for this.

main concern, as the hybrid nature of MR installations, involving physically co-located users, spaces, and artefacts as well as "virtually" co-located ones, enables complex patterns of collaborative activities.

The *Augurscope* (Figure 2.16) was an example of an MR interface for an outdoor heritage site —Nottingham Castle (UK) (Schnädelbach et al., 2002, 2006). A tripod-mounted portable display that could be freely moved and positioned overlayed a 3D virtual world of the Medieval site onto the current site, where only few traces of the original structure remain. The Augurscope supported generated live views of a virtual world on the basis of real-time changes in the physical environment (for example, other present visitors or guides would appear as avatars in the virtual world). Evaluation showed that the novelty of the installation required users to be assisted and scaffolded to some extent by researchers. Issues to do with lighting, physical placement, and accommodation of users of different heights also emerged, akin to those affecting the design of any physical installation outdoors, with changing natural light and uneven ground. An important finding was the difficulty of resolving relationships between the physical and virtual worlds, with users needing to alternatively monitor the physical and the virtual spaces, and designers needing to anticipate their movements, timings, and shifts in attention (Schnädelbach et al., 2006). The Augurscope showed that realising MR installations (which are already complex in an indoor setting) in an outdoor environment poses huge challenges, both technical and interactional.

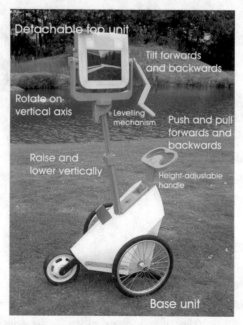

Figure 2.16: The Augurscope is a MR installation overlaying physical interaction in an outdoor heritage site with digital interaction in real time in a 3D virtual world: the user's physical interaction dynamically controlled the virtual world in real time (Schnädelbach et al., 2006) (photo courtesy of Holger Schnädelbach, used with permission).

Other MR installations explored co-visiting between people exploring a space in the physical world and in a virtual world. Galani and Chalmers (2003) ran and studied a trial of a mixed-reality co-visiting system at the Mackintosh Interpretation Centre (Mack Room) in The Lighthouse museum in Glasgow (UK). The system combined a virtual environment, a hand-held device, and tracking technology to monitor visitors' physical movements. The ambitious element of the concept was to use MR not just to deliver digital content but to mediate remote visits in conjunction with in-situ, live visits. Three visitors, one on site and two remote, could visit the Mack Room simultaneously: the on-site visitor carried a location-aware device that displayed the positions of all three visitors on a map. The off-site visitors used a web environment and a virtual environment. The virtual visitors saw a 3D first-person view with avatars representing the other visitors. All shared an open audio channel to communicate. The off-site visitors could access information on the museum holdings through delivery of web content, based on the museum's analog interpretation aids (labels, information panels, etc.). Findings were that social aspects of the visit replicated much of what is known about physical co-visiting: people pointed out interesting things to each other, gave directions and suggestions, and engaged in open discussion and anexchange of ideas. However, they needed to come up with ways to unambiguously refer to the same things so both the onsite and online visitors would understand. This indicates that interaction among companions is not strictly based on proximity but more generally on awareness of each other's activity. Real-time audio was found to be crucial for social interaction.

An example of a more didactic use of MR was *Suspended Animation, a Reflection on Calder*, an educational MR installation at the Arizona State University Art Museum created in response to a sculpture by Alexander Calder (Birchfield at al., 2008). One or two museum visitors could manipulate tangible controllers (small, soft balls illuminated from the inside) to simultaneously interact with a virtual 3D structure inspired by the sculpture, empowering visitors to "touch" and play with such a sculpture and to show the complexity of its structure and design. Evaluation showed that some visitors were reluctant to explore the physical movements that could trigger interaction. This could be explained in several ways: that they preferred limited direct interaction and onlooking, that some movements may have been uncomfortable, or with the contrast between their perception of an arts museum as a site of quiet contemplation and what the installation enabled them to do. Another finding was that interaction with the virtual sculpture often became the visitors' main focus for extended periods of time, with the physical sculpture attracting little attention. This shows that designing MR set-ups requires attention to the design of the tangible, physical elements of the installation, its contextual setting, and its relationship with the virtual component.

Aptly, MR has also been used as a framework for realising collaborative games, blending interactions in the physical and virtual world. One such example is mobile games to explore city spaces that involve participants in collecting objects and locations as well as strategising with or against other players. *Exploding Places* combines elements of historical narrative, game mechanics, and user-generated content (Flintham et al., 2011): participants could play the game at scheduled performance times in the British city of Woolwich, and could create a virtual local community and its features (such as wealth, health, and age) around significant historical events across 120 years. Facilitators in historical costumes coordinated and orchestrated the game. Due to their complexity, these MR installations require not only robust technology and extensive technical expertise, but also significant work in orchestrating the experience, with professional artists and performers contributing (Benford et al., 2011). A framework for MR performance in several contexts has been developed (Benford and Giannachi, 2011), comprising principles of digital interaction and public performance. In parallel, participants require time and support in order to take part.

While deploying such MR interactions might be beyond the ability and resources of many museums, HCI research on how interactions occur in MR settings has delivered important insights on extended reality approaches: issues with social interaction, spectator experience, orchestration and performance approaches, and issues with physical and tangible design.

2.2.3   MULTISENSORY EXPERIENCES IN MUSEUMS

Despite the words of Falk and Dierking (2013), that visitors *"devote most of their time to looking, touching smelling and listening, not to reading,"* most exhibition design focuses chiefly on the visual sense. While digital installations frequently involve sound, the other senses are less often addressed. Here lies great potential for novel designs, and both literature and practice are increasingly taking note. Levent and Pascual-Leone edited a volume on *The Multisensory Museum* (2014), exploring touch, sound, smell, memory, and spatiality, which introduces new trends in museum work, e.g., sensory activities in botanic gardens, the use of biofeedback in art, tactile museums, museums for perfume, wine, beer-brewing, coffee, chocolate, and other foods, that allow visitors to sniffle and sample, odors accompanying exhibits, olfactory artwork, and 3D printed replicas.

Immersive heritage experiences, as discussed by Kidd (2018a), rely on embodied interaction and multisensory stimulation (and site-specific narrative) to stimulate the imagination. Scenographic approaches (Bruckner, 2011) emphasise the creation of immersive architecture and sensual experiences. Bedford (2014) also suggests to take advantage of rich interactions between our senses, e.g., soundscapes that increase immersion, smell (which can trigger memories; see Obrist, 2017), movement (an example is having visitors descend a spiral, dark staircase into an ancient Egyptian tomb, turning visitors into time travelers), and other embodied experiences.

Figure 2.17: *The Interactive Tableaux* installation at the Bishops' House Museum in Sheffield used different sensory modalities. Each tableau contained a physical diorama-style scene representing a historical period. Every tableau could be activated by placing physical objects in its proximity and reacted differently: activating a sound or light, emitting a smoky smell from its frame, displaying a video on a miniature screen in the diorama, or making an automaton in the diorama move (Claisse et al., 2018) (illustration by Caroline Claisse).

In contemporary times, with the exceptions of hands-on type museums (science or children museums), touch is usually forbidden, with either human guards monitoring the galleries or proximity sensors beeping if somebody comes too close to exhibits. Most artefacts are placed behind glass, whereas in the 17th and 18th century visitors would routinely touch, shake, smell, even taste artefacts (Levent and McRainey, 2014). Some museums in the 20th century experimented with "discovery rooms" and "handling sessions" where visitors can touch and explore selected samples (e.g., in the Smithsonian Museum of Natural History). Some of the first work on touch aimed to make museums accessible to the visually impaired, with special programs that, e.g., allow exploring statues by touch. Certain museums offering extensive tactile and auditory experiences exist primarily for the inclusion of visitors with visual impairments in artistic and cultural activities: an example is the fully tactile museum Museo Omero in Ancona (Italy). Yet bodily sensation extends over touch alone, including proprioception and anticipation of touch or sensor-motor impulses when viewing art (Bacci and Pavani, 2014) as our brain integrates sensory input with motor plans, anticipating and simulating action, e.g., when seeing movement or seeing a needle pushing into a hand.

With the advent of 3D scanning and 3D printing technologies, it has become possible for museums to create replicas so that visitors can experience the shape of artefacts first-hand and experience what it is like to hold and handle them (Levent and McRainey, 2014). While such 3D printed replicas don't provide the same material properties (and thus not quite the same experience), they allow for further augmentation via inbuilt sensors and actuators or via projection (see Section 2.2.1), as they do not raise conservation concerns. A project by the Manchester Museum created a nylon replica of the limestone stela of Hesysunebef (~1600 BC), where strategically placed sensors detect touch, enabling visitors to interrogate the stela, which triggers pictures and sound files (Sportun, 2014). Harley et al. (2016) recreated medieval prayer nuts as tangible replicas, and augmented these to create reflective multisensory experiences. At three handling tables, the visitors can hold the prayer nut, smell it (it contains odor), and can see how a believer would have entered the cathedral, as a large screen reacts to how the replica is held (Harley et al., 2016; Chu et al., 2016). There is furthermore a growing movement to allow the public to "hack" and mash-up digitised artworks.[16]

Sound is already used in a variety of ways in museums, prominently with audio-guides and immersive soundscapes that bring exhibits to life and enhance visitors' imagination (Monastero, McGookin, and Torre, 2016). Sound, moreover, is an integral element for exhibitions of sound art or music museums. Control and management of sound delivery is a serious problem, as the museum itself is an acoustic space. Neighbouring exhibits may also emit sound and sounds bleed across areas, potentially resulting in a cacophony; walls create an echo and different material choices modulate sound differently. When designing interactive exhibits with significant sound components, it is thus essential to consider the final surroundings, and to test and revise audio components in-situ.

Multiple sensory modalities can be very important as part of digital interactions in settings where sensory immersion is part of the heritage experience. An example are historic buildings, where the smell of old furnishings, the texture of floors and carpets and the sounds echoing through the building all convey a sense of history and past lives. The interactive exhibition design at a house museum described by Claisse et al. (2018) incorporated not only tangible, but multisensory interaction and storytelling. Designer Caroline Claisse developed two tangible, multisensory exhibitions for the Bishops' House in Sheffield (UK): a building dating back to the 16th century that was inhabited until the 1970s and is now a community-run museum. In *Containers of Stories*, the volunteers who work at the House were represented by small cabinets. Each cabinet contained several bespoke objects telling a story selected by the volunteer. Visitors could manipulate the objects (enjoying their sensory qualities), and when placed on top of the cabinet, an auditory narrative recorded by the volunteer would play. In the *Interactive Tableaux*, several interactive mixed-media diorama-style portraits were placed across the house. Each tableau represented a historical period in

---

[16] See http://www.3Dprinter.net/mashing-up-museum-art-at-the-met.

the life of the house and a character that might have lived there at that time. The tableaux reacted to the visitor's presence in different ways by playing sound, music, visuals (light configurations, a short video, etc), operating a small automaton, or emitting smoke and smell (see Figure 2.17). Evaluation of both exhibitions shows that visitors greatly appreciated the multisensory aspects of the experience, not only because of the pleasantness of the objects and portraits, but also because it deeply resonated with the embodied experience of place while exploring the ancient house, which is one of the most memorable aspects of visiting the museum (Claisse et al., 2018).

Multisensory interactions have also been introduced in the context of more traditional art museums. A notable example is the *Sensorium* exhibition at Tate Britain (London) (Davis, 2015), where the visit to a number of paintings in the museum was complemented by specially designed multisensory content to resonate with the themes and aesthetics of the artworks (such as multi-channel sound, haptics, and olfactory displays). Francis Bacon's painting *Figure in a Landscape* was complemented by an ambient soundscape and an olfactory display of bitter chocolate. When in front of *Full Stop* by John Latham, visitors could hear the sound of a heavy downpour, and use a haptic device that used focused ultrasound to make the visitor's hand feel the sensation of rain falling upward onto their fingertips (Vi et al., 2017).

Multisensory displays and interactions have great potential to convey evocative narratives around art and heritage, although they require a high degree of bespoke work to be effective in their intended setting. While some sensory modalities (such as sound) can be designed more easily through existing, robust technologies and platforms, others—such as haptics and olfactory displays—are still very much under exploration and development.

2.3   INTERACTION BEYOND THE PHYSICAL VISIT

In some instances, interactivity can extend beyond the frame of the physical visit, either by virtue of the interaction on-site affecting off-site experiences (for example online), or by generating outcomes (such as souvenirs) of the visit that can then be used to unlock further interactive content (on return visits, or at other connected physical sites). Museums and cultural bodies have long debated and experimented with ways to entice visitors to establish a connection to the institution before they arrive and to maintain it after they have left, to repeat their visit, to access additional resources (often online), and in general to capture the impact of the visit long-term[17] regarding recall, learning, emotional identification, and entertainment value, but also on health and well-being (Lackoi et al., 2016). Literature on this topic includes studies of how people prepare for heritage visits and how they reflect on these later, as well as studies looking at longer-term learning effects (Stevenson,

---

[17]   https://www.nationalmuseums.org.uk/media/documents/publications/cultural_impact_final.pdf,
https://www.sciencecentres.org.uk/documents/60/impact-of-science-discovery-centres-review-of-world-wide-studies.pdf.

1991; Anderson, Storksdieck, and Spock, 2007). Here, we limit the discussion to aspects relevant to HCI in museums and to the interaction frames described so far: that is, how interactivity extends parts of the visit into the rest of people's lives.

Figure 2.18: Visitors may prepare and plan their museum visit so as to focus on exhibits they are particularly interested in. Technology can then be used to track the visit and to "bookmark" objects of interest. Visitors may receive a souvenir of their visit, such as a personalised postcard, and later-on can access detailed information about the topics and exhibits they expressed interest in (illustration by Katharina Bartholomäus).

Pre- and post-visit integration often features in digital interactive installations in museums. An example are mobile apps offered by museums that help plan your visit and even anticipate some of the content (for example through previews of the galleries), and to which you can go back after the visit to access further functionality. This is enabled by the BYOD model, where the means of accessing interactive content remain with the visitors on their own devices. However, research shows that only a minority of visitors agree to download museum apps, and that even a smaller minority access them again after the visit.[18]

In other cases, the post-visit interaction occurs through accessing digital online exhibitions, which are often connected with physical museum exhibits. For example, some museums give visibility to their online exhibits (which may feature holdings not on display in the physical exhibits) through interactive stations placed in the galleries, so to encourage visitors to explore them further at home. Digital exhibits can offer direct links to what was seen in a physical exhibit or offer additional content and activities to encourage longer engagement. The Victoria and Albert Museum in London have a strong strategy for this, providing companions to the visit that encourage further engagement: for example, micro-sites accompanying an exhibition of textiles offer patterns from

---

[18] https://theconversation.com/augmented-reality-promises-to-rescue-dying-museums-so-why-dont-visitors-want-to-use-it-107845.

their own archives for visitors to recreate the designs, and often to also upload their own original patterns and ideas.

However, research has shown that people need strong motivations for going back via apps or websites (these can be rewards or discounts), and that the number of people accessing post-visit activities online or on apps is a small subset of those who visited (Hornecker and Stifter, 2006b; Petrelli et al., 2017). Therefore, planning for a connection between interaction on-site and on-line might not always produce the desired results. These strategies seem marginally more successful when targeting visitors who intend to visit again, e.g., members of a loyalty programme, people local to a museum, or visiting again for other reasons (multiple school-trips or multiple visits to the same city/destination). In these cases, personalisation strategies implemented in apps or through visitor profiles on institutional websites can encourage repeat visits both on site and beyond. One approach is to let people know that there will be something new for them to see or experience. Recommendations can also be tailored for repeat visitors, for example via an app that tracks their visits. The Dallas Museum of Art runs a successful Friends programme[19] incorporating some of these features, including the link to marketing initiatives aimed at members (multiple check-ins via the app at the museum granted them discounts, vouchers, etc). Social media can play an important role in tying in to the physical visit, as we saw in some of the examples in Chapter 2.

Another approach to link to post-visit activities is that of installations that generate souvenirs of the visit that people can take away. Previous research on theme parks found that people do place value in souvenirs (and therefore tend to keep them) when their production is considered an integral part of the visitor experience and not an add-on (Durrant et al., 2011). Souvenirs can take various forms: digital (special content online that can be accessed via a code), hybrid (i.e., physical objects that enable links to digital features), or physical objects or mementoes that somehow represent a person's visit. In the exhibition *The Hague and the Atlantic Wall* (part of the meSch project), the replica objects that visitors used to access digital content at various points of the exhibit could be used at a final station to print a unique postcard. The postcard visually depicted each visitor's path (via a series of stamps representing the stations where they had stopped to access content), a map of The Hague showing the actual places in the city that the exhibition content referred to, and an individual URL linked to a automatically generated and personalised online exhibition (Petrelli et al., 2017). Similarly, in another meSch-created exhibition, *Voices from Forte Pozzacchio* (held at the Italian Historical War Museum in Rovereto), visitors received a unique souvenir postcard giving them a summary of the digital content they accessed. See Figure 2.19 for the souvenir cards from both exhibitions.

However, of the over 1,550 visitors to *The Hague and The Atlantic Wall* who printed a card, only 39 (2.5%) accessed the online post-visit exhibition. This is a well-known problem with post-visit engagement (digital or otherwise), which has not been yet resolved.

[19] https://mw2014.museumsandtheweb.com/bow/dma-friends/.

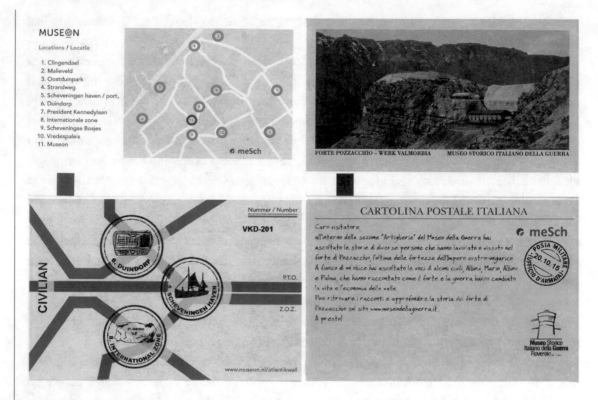

Figure 2.19: Souvenir postcards created as part of meSch project exhibitions: (left) souvenir from *The Hague and The Atlantic Wall* (Museon) displaying on the front (top) the locations in the city of The Hague corresponding to exhibition stations, and on the rear (bottom) those visited by an individual, and a unique code to access further online content; (right) souvenir from *Voices from Forte Pozzacchio* showing on the front (top) an image of the original fortress and on the rear (bottom) a personalised summary of the content accessed (postcard design by Paddy McEntaggart for meSch; photograph by Luigina Ciolfi).

Another example of souvenirs are those "materialising" aspects of the visitor experience. Nissen et al. (2014) offered souvenir-making activities to people who visited an exhibition of contemporary video art. The souvenirs took different forms, such as wristbands and small transparent domes. The design of the souvenirs was facilitated by the researchers, who made materials available to people and helped them find what best represented their experience. Nissen et al. found that souvenir making was valued as an experience in its own right and that making the souvenir helped some people make better sense of the contemporary video artworks (which many people found difficult to understand). In terms of what people felt that the souvenir would enable them to do post-visit, they mentioned that it would help them reflect on the experience of the artistic performance they saw in the videos, and give them the sense that they were extending the visit. The actual long-term impact and role of physical souvenirs in large-scale exhibitions is however difficult to evaluate, as there are very limited means to track what happens to them and their owners. Finally, another way to connect beyond the physical visit through interactivity is to design installations inspired by or linked to a museum that are meant to be experienced elsewhere, such as schools, libraries, etc. For example, the *Museum in a Box* project rents out toolkits to create interactive installations that can be designed on the basis of a museum collection.[20] Another example is the REVEAL project, which produced VR exploration games where the museum/heritage site is the backdrop of the game, to be played at the museum and at other sites (home, school, etc.) as they are freely downloadable from PlayStation VR. One such game is *The Chantry* set at Dr. Jenner's House museum in Berkeley, England.[21]

While it is an aspiration to make museum (interactive) experiences reach beyond the physical visit, this remains challenging, and an aspect of human-computer interaction work in museum that requires further research and that could benefit from insights from the field of visitor studies. It seems that strategies for sustained engagement are more effective for subcategories of visitors (e.g., enthusiasts, teachers, hobbyists who are passionate about a certain theme)—rather than when they are designed for the "general public" (Everett and Barrett, 2009; Barron and Leask, 2017).

2.4   CONCLUDING REMARKS

Interaction frames for digital interactions in museums greatly vary, and each can deliver various results depending on the type of museum, its audience, and the type of experience that is to be conveyed. Naturally, certain technological platforms are more consolidated and robust and offer opportunities for adoption (for example through toolkits—see Chapter 4) even for people without advanced technical skills; others are still very much subject of research and development. In the case of the former, the HCI field has longer experience of studying and assessing their application in heritage contexts (also due to the larger number of commercial designs that museums commission). In the case of the latter, evaluations are more often the result of controlled trials with more limited numbers of participants and shorter duration.

From our overview, a number of issues that are common to the application of any interaction frame in a museum setting were identified.

- The challenge of effectively overlaying digital content and/or behaviours over actual exhibits and spaces, so that they are complementary.

- The challenge of integrating pre- and post-visit interactions with on-site experiences in ways that complement and support each other, and that encourage visitors (or subgroups of visitors) to establish long-term engagement with the museum.

[20] http://www.museuminabox.org/.
[21] https://jennermuseum.com/2018/03/23/the-chantry/.

- The challenge of designing interactions that do not become a distraction from actual heritage holdings, i.e., striking the right balance between offering engaging interactions and monopolising the visitors' attention and focus, or of designing digital interactions so that they guide attention toward the heritage holdings.

- The challenge of designing interactions that foster learning and reflection, while also being engaging and motivating for visitors; or the trade-offs between supporting immersive engagement and the ability to reflect upon experience

- Dealing with the social nature of museum visits and reflecting on how social interaction, collaboration and cooperation (among companions or strangers) may be affected.

- The challenge of planning and delivering personalisation in ways that are appreciated by visitors and not making decisions for them that they do not appreciate. Some personalisation frames give people more flexibility to personalise the visit as they wish, while others might need explicit mechanisms to enable this.

- The importance of striking a balance between providing structure and support of activities to take place so that users understand how to use an installation, and leaving some freedom to explore and adapt.

- The challenge of designing sensory experiences that fit the topic, foster empathy and a more visceral understanding, or support imagination, when a direct experience of the heritage objects is not possible. This field has only been explored very recently, and without appropriate guidance, attempts at this might fall flat or risk creating fun-fair/amusement-park experiences.

- Content overload is always a risk and emerges within each interaction frame, either by itself (e.g., audio narratives that are too lengthy or detailed to be enjoyable; text that is too long and difficult to remember, etc.) or in concert with the rest of the exhibition (for example having too many sound or visual sources when several installations are clustered together, etc.).

- Issues to do with technical complexity are particularly critical when exploring novel technologies, which might be attractive to HCI researchers for experimentation and evaluation purposes, but on the other hand might need greater support by staff on-site for maintenance, supervision, etc. This might mean shorter-lived exhibitions and demonstrations. Technology needs to be thoroughly robust and manageable for museums to adopt for the long term. It is a common issue in HCI work in museums that prototypical installations often have a short life, limiting the opportunities for evaluation and design iterations.

• Another risk of using novel technologies is that these can quickly look dated, when visitor expectations of the quality of experiences are based on the home entertainment sector and its fast technical and narrative updates. For instance, expectations on resolution of VR experiences are due to rise quickly. It requires good content and interaction design for an exhibit to remain interesting and enticing.

• Models of storytelling that might be effective in more traditional exhibition design, or in guided tours, need to be adapted or reconsidered altogether for various interaction frames. In some cases, experts in performance, filmmaking, set, or sound design might need to be involved in order to match appropriate content and narratives to a certain interaction frame.

CHAPTER 3

Visitor Participation and Contributions

Engagement strategies promoted by cultural institutions increasingly feature participatory elements (Simon, 2010; Kidd 2014; Tallon and Walker, 2008; Clarke et al., 2015), including the possibility for visitors to respond and contribute to exhibitions in various forms. Giaccardi (2012) argues that a lively line of work on heritage as a participatory arena promotes a more comprehensive view of heritage and its importance in people's lives. Growing scholarship on participatory culture examines "(...) *how experiences, memories and identities are constructed, valued and passed on in a society in which people come together to generate, organise and share content through an ongoing interchange of thoughts and affects, opinions and beliefs, attachments and antipathies*" (Giaccardi, 2012, 6). These more active and engaged visitors constitute a new kind of heritage public: one that produces understandings and narratives as well as receiving them. On the other hand, heritage institutions are more and more aware of the added value that a dialogue with visitors, communities, and crowds can play in making museums (and interactive exhibits) more engaging (Vermeeren, Calvi, and Sabiescu, 2018)

Figure 3.1: Visitors are increasingly invited to provide feedback and to contribute (illustration by Katharina Bartholomäus).

One could argue that every form of interactivity in museums leads to some extent to visitor participation, just by virtue of giving visitors a more active role than what is normally expected of them, particularly in more traditional art museums. However, in this chapter we focus on those instances were active participation and contribution are designed to be an essential feature of digital interaction. The general goal of such an approach is to make interactive experiences less of a one-way broadcast of content and more of a dialogue where visitors have an opportunity to be active respondents, discussants, and contributors. This agency can take various forms: from becoming part of the exhibition (with their presence, or likeness, or with content they have created), to generating comments, ideas, or reactions as a response.

In the remainder of this chapter, we present various aspects of how interactivity can lead to these various forms of visitor participation and contribution. First, we discuss some key insights from curatorial strategies where visitor generate contributions (regardless of the adoption of digital technologies) that are directly relevant for HCI. Next, we examine two approaches to visitor participation and contribution via digital interactive technologies—designing bespoke interactions for participation and dialogue in museums and exhibitions—then using crowdsourcing and social media platforms for collecting inputs from large groups of participants so to become features of exhibits.

3.1   VISITOR PARTICIPATION AS PART OF CURATORIAL STRATEGIES: SOME KEY INSIGHTS

Attempts to engage visitors in active participation have been made by museums for many years, although it has always been a less-travelled path in comparison to more didactic and illustrative forms of heritage interpretation. Non-digital means to elicit visitor-generated content have been used. This includes wall displays where visitors can write their answers to questions (or comments) on the exhibition, and "wish trees" for handwritten notes, that visitors also love to browse (e.g., see Figure 3.2). Digital technologies do allow for more sophisticated forms of integrating such content as central elements of exhibits.

Figure 3.2: Trysting tree in the Robert Burns Birthplace museum in Ayreshire, Scotland. A trysting tree is a meeting place, especially for lovers. A local trysting tree featured in Burns poems was recreated in metal the museum. Visitors are invited to hang notes of love from it, imitating how lovers would leave their marks on the tree (photographs by Eva Hornecker).

More bespoke approaches often feature the work of artists using the museum as inspiration or reference, or commissioned by the museum itself to create new artistic experiences featuring the public. A recent relevant example is artist Clare Twomey's piece *Wuthering Heights—A Manu-*

script commissioned by the Brontë Parsonage Museum in Haworth, Yorkshire (UK). The original manuscript of Emily Brontë's novel *Wuthering Heights* no longer exists. Visitors to the museum during 2017 were invited to copy one line from the novel into a handmade book then exhibited during 2018, Emily Brontë's bicentenary year. The manuscript was thus collectively re-created by 10,000 people. A pencil commissioned by the artist was gifted to all participants as a tool for further writing.

Visitor experience expert Nina Simon in her books *The Participatory Museum* (2010) and *The Art of Relevance* (2016) argues that museums engaging visitors in active participation make exhibits relevant in their lives, linking to people's own experiences and values, and encouraging a long-term connection with heritage that goes beyond the physical visit. According to Simon, participatory approaches to engagement not only give visitors a voice in the context of exhibitions, but they make for overall more valuable and compelling museum experiences. While this could be seen as a call for a major change in the way a large majority of cultural institutions operate, Simon recognises that it amplifies the existing role of museums as "platforms", providers of opportunities, which is often seen as secondary in favour of their role as "educators": "*The institution serves as a 'platform' that connects different users who act as content creators, distributors, consumers, critics, and collaborators. This means the institution cannot guarantee the consistency of visitor experiences. Instead, the institution provides opportunities for diverse visitor co-produced experiences*" (Simon, 2010, p. 24). This echoes what Barbara Soren (2009) describes as "transformative" visitor experiences: "*provide new opportunities for individuals to invent personal knowledge and explore new ideas and concepts. Creating challenges in which people can discover the interconnectedness of ideas are important to personal change*" (Soren, 2009, p. 234).

On the other hand, Simon does acknowledge (and indeed separate research within HCI confirms it) that calls for active participation in museums might be off-putting for some visitors who prefer a more traditional, information-focused, and descriptive museum experience, and that therefore cannot be considered a universally effective engagement strategy. The opportunities to respond and contribute must be presented in flexible ways, giving those who do not want to engage the opportunity to enjoy the museum on their terms.

Often, public responses to events external to museums and archives can become heritage artefacts, posing challenges of how they should be curated, presented, interpreted and even archived. The Women's Library at London Metropolitan University (the largest collection of women's history in Britain, now based at the London School of Economics) in their exhibition *Iron Ladies: Women in Thatcher's Britain* made it possible for visitors to respond to the exhibition (which included materials from both the Thatcher Archive and women's organisations who were actively campaigning against Thatcherism), and this "visitors board" was an essential part of the exhibition, which touched upon a divisive period of British history (Byatt, 2005).

Grassroots campaigns born and organised on social media lead to other forms of citizen participation in historical events and how they are memorialised. Recent examples are the Jo Cox memorial wall with tributes to the British Labour MP who was killed by a far-right sympathiser in 2016 (the wall of tributes was acquired by the People's History Museum in Manchester), and the Savita Halappanavar mural and related messages representing the supporters of the Campaign to Repeal the Eighth Amendment in 2018 in Ireland, with the National Library of Ireland committed to archiving it.[22]

These examples and many of the activities that Simon sketches out in her books, and that other museum studies literature describes (McLean, 1993; Heumann Gurian, 2006; Caulton, 1998) are low-technology, but increasingly the digital has become a medium or a feature for such approaches. Indeed, enabling contributions and responses from the public has become more established in museum practice with the emergence of robust and cheap platforms for the collection of content from large groups, such as social media, and the increased popularity of personal devices that people carry with them during visits and that can be used to directly and rapidly enter content.

Beside the availability of a technical infrastructure, this approach to digital technology use for heritage has always presented challenges for heritage institutions (Kidd, 2014). One of the main issues is to do with authority and *authorship*: museums usually assume a role of authority when it comes to providing information about their holdings and to suggesting lines of interpretation (Diamond, 2005). The interpretation of a certain object on display is decided by the experts in the curatorial team on the basis of documentation, evidence, and professional expertise. Opening such a narrative to questioning or to external contributions (which might not always be factually or historically correct, or which might represent non professional—albeit informed—views) can be a profound challenge for the institution, for its staff and for how they operate, and needs careful management.

Another challenging issue is to do with ethics: opening to contributions from the public can lead to inappropriate, harmful, or offensive content being linked to an exhibition or institution, particularly when the theme of the exhibition is a difficult or divisive one. Some responses might simply be irrelevant (for instance when people leave mostly greetings) and detract from topic under discussion, as happened with the *MyRun* installation (Clarke et al., 2015). Soliciting responses requires a strategy to deal with this possibility, and to establish filtering and moderation tools and procedures that might require significant effort, as they might not be automated or completely foolproof. The use of filtering mechanisms might mean that newly authored content is not immediately "published", which is frustrating for visitors, while, on the other hand, it can be off-putting for other visitors to encounter offensive or upsetting comments in an exhibition.

---

[22] https://www.dublininquirer.com/2018/06/05/how-archives-are-changing-what-they-collect-and-when/, https://www.nytimes.com/2018/06/18/arts/design/rapid-response-collecting-ireland-berlin.html.

Visitor reactions can be enabled on-site (in an exhibition itself), or before or after the visit, and can be stored either offline on (for example) digital displays, or online on websites or social media profiles. In all these cases, the mechanisms governing the mode of contribution, the management of contributions and the boundaries and filters that might be imposed need to be decided upon specifically, and deployed and monitored accordingly.

Similar to the museums embarking on these kinds of visitor participation, HCI research in the heritage content has faced similar challenges when it comes to managing participation in interactive exhibitions. Unsurprisingly, HCI has for the majority adopted a model more akin to that of broadcasting, rather than to dialogue. However, there have been projects that have explored how digital interaction can support active visitor participation.

3.2   BESPOKE DIGITAL INTERACTIONS FOR SMALL-SCALE PARTICIPATION AND DIALOGUE

Although, as we mentioned, a participatory culture of museum interpretation has emerged on a larger scale relatively recently, bespoke applications and installations to enable visitor participation have been documented in both HCI literature and museum engagement practices for almost two decades.

Lane and Parry (2003) describe an installation to support the re-evocation and expression of personal memories of visitors at the British Museum. As part of a science and technology exhibition at The Ark cultural centre in Dublin, *Terraria* (Vaucelle et al., 2005) was designed to encourage visitors to create their own content by creating captures of their performance while playing a game. Such exhibitions allow for some degree of visitor activity and for the creation of personalised mementoes of the visit, but not for an explicit contribution of content to the exhibition itself. For example, at the National Library of Medicine's exhibit on female surgeons, visitors could create Morse code messages that could be sent to friends: while they were not used directly as a public contribution to the exhibition, engaging visitors in this activity affects the general feel of the exhibition and leaves a distinct trace (Mullen and Tuohy, 2002).

Often, the form of participation is simple and nonetheless effective. For example, at the Burns Museum in Alloway (Scotland), visitors can create a silhouette shadow portrait of themselves (see Figure 3.3), that they can email it to themselves as a souvenir (or any other email address). Portraits also appear in the installation at the museum, which is positioned next to a silhouette image of the poet Robert Burns. Seeing images created by previous visitors conveys to new visitors an idea of what the installation is about, and that they can become part of the exhibit. At the Technical Museum in Vienna (Austria), visitors could record themselves reading the news in a blue-screen TV-studio, and the recorded videos were shown in a showreel when the installation was not being used for a new recording (see Hornecker and Stifter, 2006a). These forms of participation and contribution can engender interesting instances of performativity, sense-making, and social interaction around exhibits. In both the previous examples, the installations inherently reduced the risk of "inappropriate content"—for the Burns silhouette installation via the object created (a black-white shadow-image, abstracting and anonymizing), at the blue-screen TV-studio, the setup was highly public and performative.

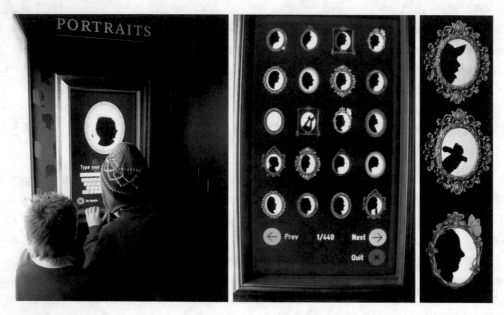

Figure 3.3: Shadow portrait installation in the Robert Burns Birthplace Museum. Papercut portraits were fashionable in Burns' times. The installation works like a photobooth. Visitors see an outline of where their face should be as well as their silhouette, and start a countdown (the camera is located on the right-hand panel). Browsing through portraits reveals creative appropriation of the medium (photographs by Eva Hornecker).

Heath et al. (2002) and Hindmarsh et al. (2002) have discussed in detail the ecologies of participation surrounding low-tech exhibits designed by artist Jason Cleverly, where visitors can visually become part of the display, such as *Deus Oculi* and *Ghost Ship*. In these examples, the participation of visitors is not in the form of comments or reactions, but in the form of populating the exhibition. In *Deus Oculi* (exhibited at the Chelsea Craft Fair in London, UK), what looked like a Renaissance painting in fact featured the faces of visitors that were captured as they were looking at other artefacts on display (which contained micro cameras). The main goal of these exhibits was to encourage and engender episodes of social interaction and communication around an exhibit, making the visitors part of the exhibit itself, and thus drawing the interest of companions and onlookers, rather than elicit content contributions or other semi-permanent traces left in the exhibition.

Another example of their work, where participation takes the form of visitor-generated creative content, is *The House of Words* exhibition at Dr Johnson House, a house museum in London (Patel et al., 2015). The exhibition included an *Interactive Work–Table and Escritoire* designed by Cleverly, where visitors were invited to contribute to a dictionary of the English language including contemporary words, a task resonating with the satirical writings of Samuel Johnson. An open book, inkwell and pen were placed on top of a writing desk (akin to Johnson's actual writing desk) in the house's attic room (Figure 3.4). However, the table was augmented with digital components, and the pen could read the handwriting and drawings of participants to transform them into dictionary entries, which were then displayed on a screen embedded into a nearby escritoire. An interesting finding from the study of how visitors participated in the installation is that the social dimension of the exhibition was enriched by the fact that the participants were aware of creating content that a wider public would view, and not just their friends or family members they were visiting with. Participants were aware of having a role in making the museum reach out of its walls (Patel et al., 2015).

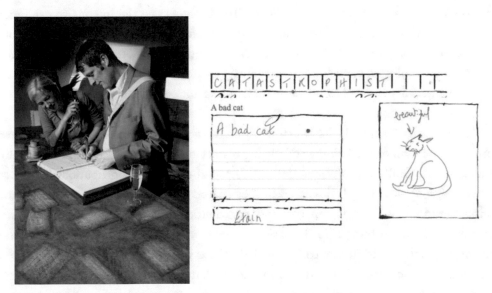

Figure 3.4: *House of Words* at Dr Johnson House Museum (London): (left) the *Interactive Work–Table and Escritoire* (design by Jason Cleverly) being used by visitors to create humorous dictionary entries; (right) a complete entry for the word "catastrophist" (photo courtesy of Dirk vom Lehn, used with permission). From Patel et al. (2015).

Ciolfi et al. (2008) have designed and evaluated several interactive installations enabling visitor contributions in various forms: in *Re-Tracing the Past* at the Hunt Museum (described in Chapter 2) visitors were invited to contribute audio recordings capturing their theories about mysterious museum objects that were never fully interpreted. These contributions were displayed on-site through an interactive radio as part of the interactive exhibition itself. In the evaluation of the exhibition, it appeared that the recordings were treated not only as traces of one's presence at the museum, but also as new sources of information to inform or inspire others' investigation of the objects. Therefore, both well-informed and plausible comments, and humorous and imaginative ones, were considered of value in shaping the overall visitor experience of the exhibition (Ferris et al., 2004; Ciolfi, Bannon, and Fernström, 2008). The recordings also worked as powerful triggers for social interaction and collaboration in the exhibition, further amplifying the performative nature of an assembly (see Chapter 2): both companions and strangers would initiate discussions while listening to previous recordings or making new ones. Another interesting finding was the role that *Re-Tracing the Past* played for the Hunt Museum Docents—volunteers who help the museum deliver its interpretation and education programmes, for example by leading guided tours and managing hands-on workshops for school children. The Docents are not trained professionals, but are Hunt Museum enthusiasts who contribute their own interests and their own independent study to guided tours and other interpretation activities. The Docents saw the interactive exhibition as an opportunity both to make more visible and to share their own work, for example by recording their own theories about the mysterious objects for others (including other Docents) to listen to. In this case, the possibility of contributing individually created content benefited not only external visitors, but a community internal to the museum that was not otherwise represented in the official visitor information.

In the interactive assembly *Reminisce* at Bunratty Folk Park, visitors were able to record audio content in relation to the holdings of a living history museum to be made available again on site and also online. Ciolfi and McLoughlin (2017) found that these contributions helped other visitors make sense of what they had seen when they arrived at the final site of the installation, the School House, and could listen to other visitors' contributions. However, they observed that the very recording of the contributions in the various cottages and houses added important elements to the visitor experience: within groups (particularly those with members from different generations), planning what to record led to discussions about family history, anecdotes, and memories; furthermore, the very activity of recording a memory shaped the experience of other visitors who happened to be in the same room, by adding a layer of personal, informal content that people could relate or react to.

Salgado and Diaz-Kommonen (2006) report on the installation *Keskustelukartta* exhibited at the Helsinki Art Museum during the Young Artists Biennale of 2005, and featuring both on-site and online components. Visitors could leave comments via an interactive screen about the exhibitions featured in the Biennale, and could also address comments and questions directly to the artists. Comments and questions engendered a dialogue among visitors past and present. Contributions were made by experts, friends, and families of the artists and by the general public, so different voices were represented in the exhibition.

Salgado et al. (2009) then developed on the findings of this research, and argue how open exhibits that enable the creation of original content can overcome the dichotomy between curators and visitors: *"We propose to use the term "community-generated content" instead, because it is the way to break open the visitors/staff dichotomy. Community-generated content is used here to refer to content produced by visitors, staff (including guards, guides, curators, educators, marketing specialists, cleaning personnel, volunteers), as well as external researchers, artists or designers."* Therefore, enabling contributions can be a way of realising an important and challenging goal that many museums and other heritage sites pursue: that of representing multiple voices in exhibitions. While this can be realised through the curatorial approach to interpretation, by proposing top-down various themes and streams of content around an exhibit, facilitating contributions can be an alternative or complementary way of achieving it, by letting various voices emerge bottom-up. Based on the evaluation of two case studies, Salgado (2008) points out that these types of installations need to be appealing in the gallery context in order to encourage people to engage with them. She proposes that installations enabling visitor responses must have a point of attraction—something that makes people want to approach and explore them; that they must enable users to directly bring about the change, giving them the sense that their contribution makes a difference and is valued; that they must be exciting, perceived as novel or surprising; that they allow for improvisation—multiple ways in which people can use them (in terms of how they configure themselves around an installation, or of how they might generate different kinds of responses); that the *end* of the interactive experience is coherent and gives a sense of continuity. Salgado proposes coherence, familiarity, multi-modality (and multilingualism), and co-experiencing as design requirements for successful participative installations (Salgado, 2008).

Another approach to creating participative interactive installation relies on an artistic approach rather than on a didactic one. One examples of this is when the heritage artefact on display is per se open to visitor participation and contributions. Sara Diamond (2005) describes new media art pieces such as Janet Cardiff and George Bures Miller's *The Paradise Institute*—a participative film installation exhibited at both the Plug In ICA in Canada and at the Venice Biennale. A second instance is when a museum is created for and is populated by newly created heritage objects contributed by the public, such as in the case of *The Silence of the Lands* (Giaccardi and Palen, 2008), a virtual museum displaying sounds contributed by individuals and communities to capture experiences of natural heritage in Colorado (U.S.) both online and on-site in specific landscapes of the area. This approach requires sustained participation and contributions, well beyond those of casual visitors exploring a museum or exhibit. Indeed, Giaccardi and Palen report how such continuous participation in the project was made possible by strong partnership with organised community groups: "*sustained community participation and meaningful life experiences are made possible through support of an active and permanent social infrastructure*" (Giaccardi and Palen, 2008, p. 287).

Figure 3.5: In the arts collection at Kelvingrove Museum, Glasgow, visitors are invited to imagine or speculate what the three people in the painting "A Marriage of Convenience" may be thinking. Here, the butler was made to think "Your wife is a dead loss, Sir. I suggest more wine," and the husband "Eye contact, make some damned eye contact!" This is a lighthearted take on visitor contribution, while encouraging interpretation of art (photographs by Eva Hornecker).

Contribution can take yet another form when the intended visitors become co-curators of exhibitions that will then include participatory elements, such as in the *Digital Natives* project (Smith and Iversen, 2014) where adolescents and young adults co-created interactive exhibitions on the theme of contemporary digital culture together with researchers and curators through a process termed *dialogic curation* (Smith and Iversen, 2014, p 256). The *Qrator* project saw visitors to the Grant Museum of Zoology (University College London) engaged in dialogue around ten exhibition cases, where they could enter thoughts and comments on iPads, representing "digital labels", or through their own devices by scanning QR codes corresponding to the exhibits (Hudson-Smith et al., 2012; Bailey-Ross et al., 2012).

A recently proposed approach to enabling contributions as a form of visitor-designed curation is that of "gifting", where a visitor's experience supported by a mobile app is not designed by curators or trained exhibition guides, but by another person (such as a friend, or a family member), and is intended to be experienced together (Fosh et al., 2014). One of the goals of this approach is to solicit contributions not to the exhibition itself, but to the interpretation layer of the visit, and to thus make interpretation itself both interactive and sociable. In the study at the Nottingham Contemporary art gallery in the UK documented by Fosh et al. (2014), a variety of experiences were designed by individuals for their chosen "visitor", from didactic ones (featuring more traditional descriptive content), to highly personal, emotionally rich ones (featuring songs with a personal shared meaning, anecdotes, etc.). The participants found the experience enjoyable, but they also noted how it can be highly prescriptive and generating a feeling of obligation—because of the effort that someone made into designing it and because that person was also present during the visit. Gifting experiences are also difficult to make available to large numbers of visitors, given the work that they entail in terms of recruiting willing "designers" and supporting them in their task of preparing a mobile narrative, which might not be appreciated.

Despite the challenges that they can pose, previous examples have shown how visitor responses and contributions are key to enlivening heritage experiences in a number of ways: enabling greater understanding through dialogue, engendering greater visitor involvement through seeing one's reactions and interventions as welcome contributions (Ciolfi et al., 2008), establishing a feeling of rapport with institutions that value visitors' input (Salgado et al., 2009), encouraging return visits and a long-term relationship between institutions and their audiences (Black, 2005, 2010), and increasing the educational and developmental value of heritage experiences (Simarro Cabrera et al., 2005; Smørdal et al., 2014).

All these examples show instances of relatively small-scale forms of visitor active contributions, relying on bespoke configurations of digital technologies and analog exhibition features. One main issues with these is their being often ephemeral, and limited to small and medium cohorts of participants.

3.3   REPRESENTING THE "WISDOM OF CROWDS": SOCIAL MEDIA AND LARGE-SCALE CROWDSOURCING

This section concentrates on how platforms supporting the participation and contribution of large numbers of participants, such as social media and crowdsourcing, can be used to introduce interactivity in museums and exhibitions. While the interaction available to people in these cases is supported by existing platform that are not bespoke for specific museums or exhibitions, and that cannot be significantly modified to suit specific purposes, the reach and availability of these tools is such that they have become important resources for enabling a certain degree of participation at scale, and involving larger groups and communities that would not be able to take part or be represented by other means. These platforms can also be used to engage people beyond the physical visit to a museum/exhibition, proposing opportunities to participate pre- and post-visit: this is an important open challenge that museums have been tackling for decades (Gammon and Burch, 2008; Hillman et al., 2012; Russo, 2011).

The increasing popularity and widespread adoption of social media platforms has had a substantial impact on the museum sector, and therefore on digital strategies to elicit visitor participation and contributions. Most heritage institutions adopt social media to some extent: they commonly have social media presence on one or more of the most popular platforms (such as Facebook, Twitter, Instagram, etc.), where they post content of various kinds—from announcements to short illustrative pieces about specific exhibits or artefacts. Hashtags dedicated to certain themes or special exhibitions are also promoted.

Many institutions also deploy social media strategies that include prompts for user reactions: for example, by encouraging people to take photos of favourite artefacts in a museum and to tweet them or share them to platforms such as Instagram. Social media applications are also used by museums to connect directly with visitors and stakeholders in more playful ways. One of the earliest experiments using social media as a way to playfully connect people to an exhibit is the @NatHistoryWhale Twitter account[23], posting "on behalf of" the blue whale model exhibited at the American Museum of Natural History in New York City. This was the first example of a museum artefact tweeting to its followers in its own "voice". In the beginning, the account was used to answer people's questions: they were encouraged to tweet to the whale during their visit, and it would answer. The account would also tweet more fun-oriented messages, such as Christmas greetings and jokes. At the time of writing, the account is operated as a more standard Twitter feed on various topics relating to natural history and heritage.

A lot of interaction via social media platforms takes place online, however it can facilitate effective connections to onsite exhibits, by encouraging people to physically visit exhibitions and by enabling some form of dialogue between onsite and online visitors and among physically co-located visitors as well (Weilenmann et al., 2013). Social media and social networking platforms have also been used by museums as part of more unusual experiments in visitor engagement on site: for example, the Art Institute of Chicago, in the occasion of their major 2016 exhibition on Vincent Van Gogh, commissioned a design agency to create a reproduction of Van Gogh's bedroom as it is depicted in his paintings of the same name as a physical room in the museum, which was then advertised both through traditional newspaper ads and leaflets in public places and on the network hospitality platform AirBnB for visitors to spend the night in, free of charge (Wohl, 2016). The use of a social platform of such reach gave huge visibility to the initiative as well as enabling the actual physical visit of people from all over the world.

Another approach to facilitating the active participation of large groups or communities is that of crowdsourcing, where contributions of knowledge, artefacts, or media are sought from the public. Therefore, work that would traditionally be performed within an organisation is outsourced to the general public or to specific targeted communities (Ridge, 2014). Members of the public can contribute by executing tasks (such as transcription or digitisation), or by providing knowledge or content. Social media and other platforms specifically designed for crowdsourcing (such as OpenIdeo for collecting design ideas, and CrowdMap for populating maps of various areas/locations) can be used as powerful tools to mobilise these efforts at scale when it comes to museums. For example, hashtags are used to encourage people to post not only comments on an exhibit or theme, but also content (such as personal photographs), thereby enabling both contributions and a

[23]   https://twitter.com/nathistorywhale?lang=en.

more complex (and even long-lived) dialogue with visitors. Crowdsourced exhibitions have existed in museum practice for decades: for example, museums often invite the public to bring in physical objects from a certain period or theme fto be exhibited, or to contribute information that will be included in a curated exhibition. A relevant example is the *Museum of Modern Nature* exhibition at the Wellcome Collection in London (2017), whereby members of the public could bring an object—any object—that represented their connection to nature. Owners of selected objects where then asked to contribute the stories behind each as the only form of interpretation in the exhibition (Meier, 2017).

Due to their popularity and reach, social media platforms have enabled these initiatives to achieve a much broader reach and greater potential engagement than it had been possible or achievable before. Ridge argues that cultural heritage crowdsourcing is more than a framework for generating content, but is a *"form of engagement with the collections and research of memory institutions, it benefits both audiences and institutions"* (Ridge, 2014, p. 2), and that it encourages skills development and deeper engagement with cultural heritage itself.

The Victoria and Albert Museum in London has successfully used social media in this way for many years: it was one of the first museums to solicit public contributions on themes relating to the permanent galleries and to special exhibitions, such as a very successful one on wedding dresses where the public were invited to "donate" digital photographs of their wedding dresses to the archive via a specially created open pool on the social photo sharing platform Flickr. The photos would feature together with dresses from the V&A fashion department. The museum is continuing this approach to planned exhibitions: for example, in 2018 they are partly crowdsourcing a planned exhibition on British fashion designer Mary Quant, using the hashtag #WeWantQuant to create a trail of the contributions that people provide (i.e., photographs of Mary Quant clothes they own) and related discussions (Kennedy, 2018; Lister, 2018). The Brooklyn Museum in New York City has adopted a crowdsourcing approach for several projects using various digital tools. A notable example not making use of social media was *Split Second: Indian Paintings* (2011).[24] The idea behind the project was that of capturing quick judgement, and the goal was to see how a person's split-second reaction to an artwork would affect their museum experience overall (e.g., what other work they approach to observe, how their opinion may change, etc.). *Split Second* started as an online evaluation where audiences were shown images of the museum's Indian paintings collection and were asked to express their preferences, views and reactions through three steps (timed trial, appeal rating, and qualitative written feedback). The results of the online study were then exhibited in correspondence to the actual paintings in the onsite exhibition at the museum.

Besides museums and other established cultural institutions, social platforms has also been instrumental for a number of grassroot heritage initiatives, where communities have campaigned and worked in support of preservation, visibility, and challenged interpretations of heritage. Ex-

[24] https://www.brooklynmuseum.org/exhibitions/splitsecond.

amples at different scale are the campaign led by the New Media Nation group in Hawai'i for the protection of the Mauna Kea site and the promotion of native Hawaiian heritage and language (Shay, 2018), and the *Saving Bletchley Park* social-media driven campaign in the UK through which the work of British codebreakers during World War II has been brought to public recognition and the site of Bletchley Park developed into the National Museum of Computing (Ciolfi et al., 2018).[25]

More often than not these activities are blurred with marketing and promotions and they might not be deemed inappropriate for all types of heritage discourse, particularly when heritage might present difficult or sensitive topics (Kidd, 2014). Heritage being often divisive or carrying difficult histories can lead to unfiltered reactions that are upsetting, or inappropriate: as a notable example, in 2014 a tweet[26] including a selfie taken by a young woman visiting the Auschwitz-Birkenau concentration camp went viral, with thousands of critical and angry reactions to the seemingly inappropriate practice of taking a selfie at such a site and sharing it. On the other hand, many argued that the selfie was a way for the person to mark an important heritage visit, and to make the site known or visible to many (younger) people who might not have known of it (Kidd, 2018b). Whatever the view on this episode, it shows both the difficulty of managing social media interactions around heritage sites or themes that are challenging and potentially sensitive, and the impact that such sharing and participative practices might have in certain cases.

Mainstream social networking platforms have a number of limitations in this respect: they have not been designed with heritage settings in mind, and they lack the flexibility to allow heritage professionals to deliver unique content narratives and to curate visitor responses in a way that is meaningful and appropriate, for instance by responding with digital assets that shed further light on the topic, or by presenting related visitors' reactions in context to each other. They lack effective and nuanced mechanisms of moderation, filtering and response. Furthermore, social media interaction often has a feel of ephemerality—the effort put into engaging audiences and the content they produce is not adequately archived, acknowledged, or maintained (Allen-Greil et al., 2011; Grabill et al., 2009; Russo, 2011). Furthermore, they have no means of connecting to existing digital heritage assets and their full metadata, making them of limited value for institutions wishing to link them to their collections.

In light of this, social sharing and visitor contributions have been, in some instances, integrated with bespoke "cultural commons" platforms, purposely designed for the heritage domain (Marttila and Botero, 2017). An example was *NaturePlus* by the Natural History Museum (London) (http://www.nhm.ac.uk/natureplus/) a bespoke system operating a crowdsourcing model to leverage the wisdom of the 'hive mind' to help construct curatorial knowledge of the natural world (Ridge, 2014).

---

[25] http://www.tnmoc.org/.
[26] Auschwitz selfie story (2014): https://www.washingtonpost.com/news/the-intersect/wp/2014/07/22/the-other-side-of-the-infamous-auschwitz-selfie/?utm_term=.f7925ee3a0f3.

On a larger scale, Europeana is perhaps the most extensive and comprehensive example: a European-wide digital aggregator, repository and display environment connecting over one thousand museums, libraries, and archives and their digital holdings, as well as spearheading many thematic projects and public participation initiatives (www.europeana.eu). In the Europeana Creative/Culture24 project *VanGo Yourself*, people were encouraged to take photos of themselves in poses recreating famous paintings and share them online (Figure 3.6).[27] The project featured many participating museums in The Netherlands, Belgium, Luxembourg, Germany, Denmark and the UK. The Europeana Migration project (2018) mixes digital and on-site activities for crowdsourcing, encouraging the public to contribute digital artefacts (photographs, stories, etc.) relating to migration and to make physical contributions through onsite "collection days" held in cities and towns across Europe.

Figure 3.6: Screenshot showing a variety of recreations of paintings from the *VanGo Yourself* project developed by Culture24 (https://vangoyourself.com/category/vango/). *VanGo Yourself* is a crowdsourcing project where people are encouraged to select an artwork from a European museum, stage their own recreation of it, and upload it to a digital gallery (via a mobile app or a web interface. Currently, 34 venues in 15 countries are participating by making images of paintings in their collection available to the project (image courtesy of Culture24).

[27] https://pro.europeana.eu/post/discover-art-in-a-whole-new-way-with-vangoyourself.

3.4   OVERALL ISSUES AND CHALLENGES

The practice of encouraging visitor responses and contributions to heritage is not as widely widespread as the success of previously described project would indicate. There are in fact several challenges to it that may discourage its take-up: notably, the effort of structuring effective frames for participation in the visit, the work required to manage, monitor and deal with the responses, and the limitations of existing tools supporting these activities, particularly digital ones.

However, a key advantage of establishing a discussion with heritage holdings is the benefit that this brings to the social and collaborative aspect of the visit: encouraged to respond, visitors will also discuss among themselves as well as with the institution and the social aspect of heritage will increase both online and onsite, which is a very desirable outcome for heritage institutions.

Despite this, few cultural institutions have comprehensive strategies for facilitating visitor contributions and visitor generated content. Furthermore, most institutions leave visitor generated content that might be generated around an exhibition in the medium the content is collected with, such as the CMS of a website, which was neither made for this purpose nor designed to treat incoming responses as possible assets for preservation. This means that the efforts of encouraging responses might not lead to tangible outcomes for museums in terms of new knowledge generated, and historical accounts of these initiatives.

Enabling visitor contributions can be daunting, particularly with regard to difficult heritage and challenging histories, as we saw earlier in the episode of the "Auschwitz Selfie". Many institutions may not have the resources, time or expertise to moderate, filter or respond to instances of inappropriate responses, although—as we saw—an increasingly widespread culture of social sharing means that any forms of monitoring that institutions might deploy, are necessarily limited.

Common findings show that the success of digital engagement initiatives based on visitor responses/contributions is linked very much to how the activity of contributing and generating responses is framed within a meaningful and immersive narrative. The visitors' willingness to respond is greater if it makes sense to respond in the context of the experience and if it looks like it will have an impact on the heritage and on others. Setups that require little effort to contribute and where visitors do not feel under pressure to be "creative" or to perform publicly can be just as successful as setups that are more challenging, but in the latter case, the experience needs to be rewarding and enticing enough for visitors.

All of the examples we described in this chapter respond to the re-articulation in the last decade of museums as *fora*: meeting places where visitors' narratives and experiences are valid and valued. They do so in a way that complements rather than challenge the traditional work of the institutions, creating (for example) opportunities to identify artefacts and gather knowledge. Previous research has demonstrated that being prompted to contribute to heritage experiences *can* lead to greater memorability, learning and prolonged engagement (Ciolfi et al., 2008; Ciolfi and McLoughlin, 2012; Salgado, 2008; Hindmarsh et al., 2002; Walker, 2008).

CHAPTER 4

The Development Process

Poor design can result in broken exhibits—visitors either do not know how to use an exhibit and think it is broken, or they unintentionally break things (Kollmann, 2007). Besides usability and apprehendability (so visitors know within a few seconds how to interact), good design requires good choice and design of content so that it appeals to visitors. This foregrounds the importance of the development process. In the following, we first discuss how user-centred design approaches can inform this process, and then discuss co-design approaches, which involve users (both staff and visitors) actively. Moreover, we discuss DIY (Do-It-Yourself) approaches: that is, toolkits that enable cultural heritage professionals to build interactive installations, and thereby reduce reliance on technical experts and companies. In this case, the focus of the development process is not on finished installations, but on providing tools and support to enable curators to realise their own.

Figure 4.1: The development of new installations usually proceeds from initial concept development over iteration of prototypes to the final version to be installed in the museum (illustration by Katharina Bartholomäus).

When developing installations to be put into a museum, we have to take into account how museums normally develop exhibits and exhibitions, and how this drives their expectations. There are three main approaches used by museums—from conceiving, designing, and constructing all exhibits in-house, to conceiving them in-house and then handing over to contractors, to all steps being conducted by contractors (Clarke, 2013; Maye et al., 2014). As many museums do not have much technical staff, the first approach is rare (often limited to museums with large numbers of staff and a need to work in-house, for example due to scheduling, or the frequency of changing/updating/ extending exhibits).

Some museums are very open to working with academics and students (in particular museums that lack the resources to contract design companies or freelancers), while others are more apprehensive, since academics might not be able to present a portfolio of past works and references from other museums, and their pace of work might not fit the museum's plans or priorities. Moreover, academic projects often are more conceptually driven or technology oriented, whereas many design companies iterate on successful patterns of exhibition design.

When working with museums, it is important to develop good relationships with museum staff and management, in particular when aiming to establish partnership (particularly in the long-term), or when doing something innovative that might require curators to embrace different ways of engaging visitors or to—at least partially—give up on curatorial control (see Chapter 3 on visitor contributions). Moreover, curators and other professionals working in museums (such as exhibition designers and interpretation officers) have much to bring to the table, and thus designers benefit from finding out existing expertise and motivations of cultural professionals. Lastly, the concerns of museum professionals are sometimes essential, for instance regarding adequate storage and handling of artefacts. Given that it can take considerable effort to establish a good working relationship, these can be fruitful for long-term collaboration and for subsequent projects. We will touch on this in the following sections.

4.1   USER-CENTRED DESIGN

In User-Centred Design (UCD, see call-out box on next page), "users" have the role of both informants (from whom to gather requirements, needs, and wishes) and "targets" (who will use the final design). Their involvement is usually sought mainly at the requirements definition and the evaluation stages, whereas in co-design (see next section) users take a much more prominent role in the actual design activity. A user-centred approach to exhibit development follows similar steps as in other domains of HCI, appropriating and adapting these to the museum and heritage context. Given UCD methodology is considered conventional in HCI, it is rare to find explicit descriptions of UCD-driven development processes for museum installations in the literature, which tends to focus on design rationale and evaluation outcomes. Still, a UCD approach needs to be concretised, and we here briefly address elements to be considered for the museum context. For a more thorough introduction, we advise investigating textbooks on UCD, interaction design and the HCI design process (Benyon, 2013; Buxton, 2007; Goodman et al., 2012; Sharp et al., 2019).

User-Centred Design

User-Centred Design (UCD) entails an iterative design process of systems. It does not rely on a "genius" designer (most geniuses actually rely on extensive experience, including that of failed projects, etc.) but follows a principled approach of investigation (so to identify design requirements), idea generation, and testing in order to create systems that are usable, useful, as well as suitable for the context of use.

Initially, a holistic understanding of task requirements, user characteristics, and usage context will be sought, often via empirical investigation. Design concepts are developed on this basis and, over time, turned into (first simpler and later more complex and finalised) prototypes. These concepts and prototypes are evaluated with potential users, which determines how concepts and prototypes should be improved and may also give rise to further investigation to address knowledge gaps. This results in a spiral of study-design-evaluate-(study)-design-evaluate (etc.) until the final outcome is determined to be adequate (or, pragmatically, time and other resources run out). Early testing of concepts, including that of sketches and other forms of envisionments is key to UCD. Further keystones of UCD are involvement of users when determining requirements and in evaluation, as well as the iterative process.

UCD utilises a wide range of methods throughout this process, some taken from social sciences, others from design disciplines and human factors. This includes, for instance: contextual enquiry, interviews, observation, stakeholder analysis, personas, scenarios, paper-prototyping, video prototyping, user testing, field studies, etc.

Requirements analysis should investigate and enquire the factors discussed in Chapter 1, such as the type of museum and its aims, expected visitor demographics, the type of content to be communicated, and the physical environment the exhibit will be placed in and how it will integrate in this. As a simple example, one should keep in mind noise conditions and light levels, where surrounding exhibits may influence the visitor experience. It is becoming more common to work with directional audio (where the audience can only hear the audio in specific positions) to avoid noise pollution and interference between exhibits. Empirical methods used for requirements analysis are referred to as "front-end evaluation" in institutional audience research (Kelly, 2004; Davies and Heath, 2013).

Figure 4.2: Prototyping and user testing go hand in hand in UCD. The initial concept for a painting installation for children was tested in paper form with two participants to determine if the interaction concept was understood. Then, a half-functional mockup was created and tested by 16 adults. It had a touchscreen inserted, and a facilitator-wizard could remote-control the selection of animals and paint colour in response to users' actions. A second, improved version of this was evaluated with two children. An interim development prototype used a rear-projection, where the final system had a touchscreen as surface again (Clarke and Hornecker, 2012, 2015) (photo courtesy of Loraine Clarke).

Understanding visitor demographics helps to determine which audience(s) to address, which interests and experiences these already bring in, how to tailor content, and which forms of interaction and aesthetics will be appealing. It can be useful to do stakeholder analysis, considering secondary and tertiary stakeholders, which are easily forgotten. This concerns any staff involved in technical maintenance, daily housekeeping (e.g., switching installations on and powering them down), or content updates. Furthermore, floor wardens are often approached by visitors if installations are difficult to use, or need to keep watch over installations that are fragile and where pieces might get lost. Various established UCD techniques from HCI can be applied in the museum context to determine design requirements. This includes focus groups (with visitors or experts), interviews with staff and audiences, and observations. For instance, AMARC (Australian Museum Audience Research Centre) did five focus group sessions in preparation for an exhibition on the topic of Death, to understand attitudes to the theme, interest, and expectations, and guidance for suitable content that was not "too gruesome" (Kelly, 2004).

As part of the UCD process it is essential to iterate in order to improve system design, or, in earlier stages, to compare and evaluate alternative concept designs. It is advised to follow iterative procedures for prototyping and testing, starting with simple mock-ups and continuing to interactive prototypes with increasing functionality and refined design. Any appropriate method from paper prototyping to Wizard of Oz prototyping (where a moderator remote-controls the system, providing the illusion of a working system) and bodystorming (a creative method that adapts and extends brainstorming, based on direct improvisation and acting out ideas) may be utilised. Concept design and prototyping may be scenario-driven (Torpus, 2018). In our own work and collaborations with museums we have come to learn that it is important to anticipate scale and physical setup in prototyping. For instance, while a small-scale mockup might provide insights into interaction and appearance of an installation, it can be difficult to recreate the effect that scale has on lines of sight, physical layout, and crowdedness, or for how accessible an installation is for people of different heights and sizes. When testing an interactive tabletop, its size will influence how many people can surround it and interact, which might influence interaction patterns, and screen size can also affect usability in terms of how easy it is to read and select items.

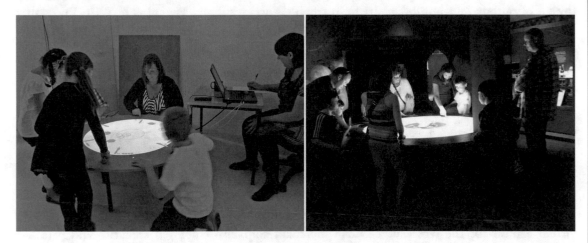

Figure 4.3: To emulate the future setup and social situation for a museum tabletop game, we built a table of adequate size that we projected onto and then invited families to "play". A facilitator started the software and took notes; the sessions were also video-recorded. While the final installation is larger, the social interactions were similar, and the user tests helped identify various usability and understanding issues (Hornecker and Nicol, 2011) (photographs by Eva Hornecker).

Unfortunately, literature on how to evaluate museum installations as part of an iterative design process (formative evaluation) is rare. Most publications focus on summative evaluation. This is partially because most iterative design processes as conducted by museums themselves or commercial companies are rarely documented in publications, and also because UCD processes are considered "normal" in HCI research, so publications will instead focus on insights regarding design features, rather than the design process and prototype testing.

Maquil et al. (2017) discuss the iterative design process for *BatSim*, a tangible interface embedded in a workbench (see Figure 2.8), supporting playful discovery of methods for creating batteries, for the Tudor Museum, which is dedicated to the science of electricity and Henri Tudor, inventor of the lead accumulator. The team started by analyzing the current exhibit via a cognitive walkthrough and interviews with a curator. In conjunction with knowledge on the audience and insights from the literature, this led to defining design goals and learning aims for a revised exhibit. The design process involved three prototypes, starting with a paper prototype that reflected the sizes and shapes of envisioned components in order to test sizes and spatial configuration. This was tested in a design workshop with small groups, giving insights on how to best distribute components on the workbench so as to enable group collaboration. The next prototype was functional, built from cardboard with embedded conventional displays and various electronic elements, so as to enable testing the interaction flow. A third high-fidelity prototype detailed form and feedback and was tested in the museum. This led to another iteration, which finalised the physical design, graphical design of output, and improvements to instructions and feedback. Maquil et al. (2017) note that the functional prototypes were important for refining interaction metaphors, exploring interaction techniques, test interactions, and, with a more refined version, evaluate the system feedback, ensuring apprehendability. Torpus (2018) and his team began each of three projects by defining criteria catalogs and requirements, then developed scenarios together with the museum partners (an excavation of a roman trade centre, a farmhouse in an open air museum, and a cultural museum) and professional design agencies involved. These scenarios were then used for a walkthrough with external participants, to further analyse the concept design and anticipate any problems as well as identify opportunities. Once first prototypes were developed, usability studies in a lab setting were run, focusing on general issues such as comprehensibility, discoverability, and the potential of the technology to augment physical exhibits. Reunanen et al. (2015), who developed an immersive virtual exhibit for the wreck of a Dutch merchant ship, also employed scenarios and personas early-on to envision visitor groups and their interaction with the exhibit. Role-playing and acting out scenarios as performance helped to identify further requirements and issues. Later, the Wizard of Oz technique was utilised to test different metaphors for gestural interaction with the 3D environment, where an observer identified gestures and then navigated the 3D model. Incremental prototyping and testing further refined the navigation concept, which was then evaluated in a lab setup anticipating the final exhibition setting.

One of the best-documented examples for formative evaluation is the kind of iterative A/B testing and design iteration done by the SF Exploratorium, where even instructional guidance is often A/B tested for which version triggers more learning-related dialogue (Dancstep et al., 2015), with different versions of an exhibit alternated over several weeks on the museum floor (sometimes replacing exhibit titles and slogans, sometimes altering the exhibit design). This requires a fully working system that can be used without staff support, which for digital exhibits is hard to achieve at prototyping stage.

Another approach is to recruit volunteers (often there is a "friends of XY" mailing list) for a testing session. Approaches from usability testing can be adapted (see e.g., Hornecker and Nicol, 2011, 2012), keeping in mind the non task-oriented mindset of visitors and visitor demographics. Participants may be told to "play" or "just explore", depending on the type of activity facilitated by the system, and one may invite family or friend groups to take part in evaluation sessions. Such studies are useful in revealing obstacles to immediate apprehendability and factors that frustrate users or result in an unsatisfactory experience, delivering hints for improving the system. Still, actual usage is hard to predict, given it is influenced by many factors, including placement of (other) exhibits, overall spatial constellation, and by the fact that people behave differently in the free-choice situation of a museum visit compared to taking part in what they know to be an evaluation study (see Hornecker and Nicol, 2012). Usability studies combined with interviews and questionnaires, as described by Hornecker and Nicol (2011), can also help to improve phrasing (of labels, buttons, instructions, help text), by asking participants to describe what they did, liked or didn't like, imagine how they would explain to others what they did, or what they understood and learned. This can be used to derive phrasing that is closer to visitor's experience and pre-understanding.

Figure 4.4: Whether or not visitors will understand how to interact and will engage in the hoped-for conversation and interaction patterns can often be tested with simplified, small-scale models (photo courtesy of Loraine Clarke).

Some museums already use approaches related to UCD. For example, one of the institutions we have collaborated with, the Glasgow Riverside Transport Museum, tends to provide contractors with a detailed brief or "interpretation plan" (Clarke, 2013). This includes what the "story" is, the key message, target audience, and desired learning outcomes: (1) knowledge and understanding; (2) skills; (3) values, attitudes and feelings; (4) creativity, inspiration and enjoyment; and (5) behaviour. Such an interpretation plan might describe that an exhibit is aimed at families and school field trips, that it is expected that they visit in groups, that the exhibit aims to raise an interest (e.g., in how steam trains function), and the awareness of how this is a collaborative task, and would describe the exhibit activity as collaborative and challenging. Curators and technical staff often discuss potential technological platforms before handing out the brief, and may even develop a paper prototype and test it with "friends of the museum" before contracting a company.

Formative prototyping and testing are also useful in terms of relationship building with the museums. They are opportunities for museum staff to witness (or become aware of) the progress of a project, and to be asked for their views and input as experts who know how visitors approach certain spaces/exhibits. If a certain interactive exhibit requires regular maintenance or housekeeping by museum staff, these are also opportunities to evaluate the mechanisms by which these functions will be performed, and their own usability and clarity.

4.2   CO-DESIGN AND PARTICIPATORY APPROACHES

Participatory Design (often also called **Co-Design**) originated in Scandinavia in the 1970s as an approach to include citizens and workers in design and decision making regarding public facilities, services for housing or in workplaces. Participants are full design partners (rather than informants or testers) and have an active role in contributing and making decisions during the design process. Their concerns, wishes, and needs are represented directly and persistently in design teams, rather than being confined to dedicated phases of consultation as in UCD.

This approach has been adopted for the design and development of computer systems supporting work (Greenbaum and Kyng, 1991) and of other interactive experiences, such as platforms for public participation and consultation (Bratteteig and Wagner, 2010). Participatory Design (PD) has proven to increase successful adoption of novel digital systems in various work contexts (where end-users' awareness that they have contributed to the systems supports processes of innovation and organisational change) and to generate positive relationships among stakeholders. PD is an established approach in HCI, and for many years has been applied beyond work settings to include the cultural heritage domain.

When discussing PD in the context of HCI for museums, it is important to consider who participates in the design process, given the variety of stakeholders: visitors (particularly if focusing on specific audience sub-groups), museum staff (with various specific skills and responsibilities), and other stakeholders such as boards of management, community volunteers, local authorities, schools, etc. In PD, representatives of various stakeholder groups bring their concerns and knowledge to the discussion table: they can be insights on the physical environment that the technology will be placed in (which, as we saw, should be a primary concern also in a UCD process), but also other factors such as institutional strategy, ethical considerations and audience understanding.

An early example of adopting participatory elements in HCI work for museums is reported by Broadbent and Marti (1997): participatory workshops with stakeholders for envisioning scenarios for technology in a museum housed in a historic building, with representatives from museum staff, the local authority, the tourism office, etc. (Broadbent and Marti, 1997). Examples of HCI research in museums adopting a full co-design approach include instances where visitors were part of the design team. Taxén (2004) conducted a co-evaluation of exhibits at the Museum of Science and Technology in Stockholm (Sweden), and led co-design of digital interaction concepts with visitors for the Vasa Museum (also in Stockholm). Co-design can also engage specific categories of visitors: Dindler et al. (2010) worked with children and adolescents in designing interactive games for playful interactions, and in Smith and Iversen's (2010) *Digital Natives* project, the content of an interactive exhibition was collaboratively designed with teenagers. This work is part of a larger research programme for the greater involvement and agency of children in participatory processes (Iversen, Smith, and Dindler, 2017). Another example is Roussou et al.'s (2007) work where children co-designed an educational program supported by digital technologies.

In other cases, co-design processes focus on participation of cultural heritage and museum professionals. Our own work on the meSch project is a notable instance: museum curators, exhibition designers and education and engagement officers were full members of the co-design team that generated not only a series of interactive installations, but a technology design toolkit aimed at cultural professionals as main users (Petrelli et al., 2013).

Fuks et al. (2012) report on another instance of co-design of collaborative technologies in museums, with the participation of both staff and visitors; however, the outcomes were interaction concepts and prototypes, rather than fully operational interactive exhibits.

The involvement of these various actors in a participatory design process needs careful planning and management: it can lead to fruitful relationships and effective design outcomes, but also demands substantial efforts from facilitators and coordinators. Issues to consider include: who the facilitator is, which stakeholders participate, and how they participate. Even when attempting to work as equal partners and contributors, problematic issues and tensions in terms of power dynamics can emerge, including personal interrelationships and decision making (Vines et al., 2013; Bratteteig and Wagner, 2014). There can be diverging, or even conflicting interests in the team, which need facilitation and mediation: for example between museum curators focused on preservation and educators focused on learning outcomes, or community representatives advocating for cultural resources and local authorities with tight budget constraints, etc.

Figure 4.5: In the meSch project, museum curators, exhibition designers, and education and engagement officers were full members of the co-design team. Co-design workshops were held where designers, developers and museum professionals generated together interactive concepts and scenarios. In this instance, the workshop was held at the Museo Storico Italiano della Guerra in Rovereto (Italy), and the participants were surrounded by museum artefacts in support of brainstorming while developing design ideas together (photograph by Eva Hornecker).

Another aspect to consider is commitment on the part of participants: for stakeholders, being part of a participatory process means investing a greater length of time and more substantial effort in being part of the work than with a UCD process. Therefore, it is important to carefully discuss expectations, and be realistic and honest in terms of what the demands on participants will be. It can be a challenge to realise co-design in the heritage domain as it is a field that often suffers from limited resources, and where staff can find it difficult to add to their already substantial responsibilities that of being part of a design process. Similar concerns apply when involving volunteers and local communities who already volunteer their time and skills and are asked to give time to additional activities. For all these reasons, it is important to clarify the potential benefits and outcomes for those involved: in terms of the final result (e.g., interactive experiences that represent their views and contributions), but also in terms of what can be learned and gained from the process itself (Avram and Ciolfi, 2019).

In these partnership, recognising who is able (and even expected) to make decisions, and at which stages of the process, is extremely important as it is a critical jointure of the PD process. This is key to establish as part of the negotiation and communication between stakeholders, and so are mechanisms for consensus building toward decisions. For instance, it is important in collaborative and participatory processes to respect the different expertise and kinds of agency that different stakeholders may have within a project. However, certain hierarchies from management structures can halt decision making and undermine participatory processes if this is not clearly understood at the planning stage.

Another challenge considers how the co-design process should be structured, as it can shape how ideas are developed and to what extent they are agreed upon. An important aspect is the role of prototypes and proofs-of-concepts: often, novel technologies and interaction frames are explored, and it can be challenging for heritage stakeholders to envision their application and development, the novel technologies and user experiences these can provide (Ciolfi et al., 2016; Halloran et al., 2006). Designers and technical experts, on the other hand, can find it difficult to recognise some of the barriers to experimentation that heritage stakeholders might perceive or might be dealing with. Prototypes can be very useful as shared artefacts that bridge between members of a co-design team with different skills, expectations, and priorities. At the same time, they can sometime hinder creativity and innovation as participants might be reluctant to discuss different interaction concepts and ideas once an existing prototype is seen as particularly interesting and effective, particularly if it is a fairly developed and polished prototype.

One possible approach for sustaining and facilitating a participatory process is for the HCI researcher to actively contribute to a museum as a volunteer. Many museums (especially in the UK and U.S.) have volunteer programmes open to enthusiasts and members of local communities. By volunteering, researchers can demonstrate their commitment to the institution, and thereby encourage members of staff and other volunteers to commit in turn to a participatory design process. Furthermore, researchers can gain more in depth knowledge of the institution and how it operates, which can greatly help facilitate and coordinate the process. For example, Claisse volunteered at the Bishops' House museum in Sheffield (UK) (Claisse, Ciolfi, and Petrelli, 2017), to engage other long-term volunteers from the local community in the co-design of multisensory tangible interactive installations to be exhibited at the house (discussed in Chapter 2). In her work, the specific goal was for the technology to give visibility and voice to the community of volunteers. Another example is that of Maye, who volunteered at the Hunt Museum in Limerick (Ireland) to study how digital technologies are adopted and applied in the museum as well as to facilitate the co-design of novel visitor aids (Maye et al., 2017). While this approach can be beneficial in terms of rapport building and process facilitation, it also demands substantial effort and time commitment on part of the researcher, and might not be feasible in every circumstance. Furthermore, it might create some blurring or confusion of the role that the researcher holds in the co-design team, for example being a member of the museum community but also an HCI expert, technologist, etc..

A number of methodologies and techniques can be employed as part of the co-design process: creative workshops, walkthroughs, role-play, and cultural probes. Workshops are a popular technique as they can bring all participants together, and enable them to plan for dedicated time to give to the process, rather than fit project-related activities into their daily work. However, facilitators will need to devise strategies to sustain the participatory process between moments of in-presence work and discussion. Approaches used include shared blogs (where all participants jointly document the process), regular virtual meetings, and dedicated groups on social media platforms.

Some of the examples we mentioned above represent very successful instances of participatory design for the heritage sector (Iversen, Smith, and Dindler, 2017; Claisse, Ciolfi, and Petrelli, 2017; Petrelli et al., 2013), and this seems to be linked to how well the process enabled the representation of stakeholders' concerns and ideas, a sense of accomplishment and ownership, and a shared buy-in of the museum's ethos and qualities. A note of caution, however, relates to the commitment and effort that participatory processes demand (thus adopting co-design might not necessarily be possible or suitable in every case), and also to the challenges of shared decision making. Moreover, design and domain expertise should always guide realisation of the final outcome. Sometimes it can be difficult for participants in a participatory process, who over time become experts in the exhibit concept developed, to envision what it would be like for first-time users, or to imagine how the installation might fit into the larger context of the museum and the social configuration of museum visiting. The interaction concept championed by representatives of potential visitor groups may turn out to be too complex for the general public (for instance resembling a complex video game, which needs time to learn). The role of experts and facilitators is therefore key. This reiterates the importance of effective facilitation and coordination of a co-design team, and of establishing a clear agreement over areas of expertise, and well as over a formative evaluation plan.

4.3   DIY APPROACHES: SUPPORTING MUSEUMS TO AUTHOR INTERACTIONS

Do-It-Yourself (DIY) approaches are increasingly popular, where technical experts and/or HCI designers realise platforms, or toolkits, which are then appropriated and utilised by end-users (e.g., museum staff, exhibition designers, etc.) in the creation of digital projects. This approach emerges from lines of research in End User Development—creating tools supporting users, who may have little to no specialised technical knowledge, to design novel technologies (Lieberman et al., 2006), and meta-design, the creation of open systems or environments that users can shape to suit their creative practices (Giaccardi and Fischer, 2008). Such platforms/toolkits are sometimes developed in a UCD approach, and in other cases through a participatory approach.

Figure 4.6: The meSch Internet of Things (IoT) Toolkit: server, projector, printer, sensors, and mobile device running the editing environment (physical toolkit design and photograph by Nick Dulake, Design Futures).

Cultural heritage professionals may be interested in toolkits that enable them to develop museum installations for various reasons (Petrelli et al., 2013; McDermott et al., 2013). Usually, cultural heritage institutions rely on having a technology department (which only large institutions can afford) or on outsourcing development to external companies or freelancers. DIY toolkits can enable in-house development by non-technology experts and thus significantly lower costs. Moreover, they thereby retain control over the system design and, perhaps even more importantly, are able to update contents when needed, which is something that typical maintenance contracts usually exclude, or is too costly to afford for museums.

Several toolkits have been built for the heritage domain over the years, with various take-up and impact on institutions. Early examples focused on VR and AR. An early example was ARCO (Sylaiou et al., 2008). ARCO was for the development of virtual exhibitions embedding 3D virtual objects and galleries, to be experienced either remotely, on the Web, or at information kiosks in the museum. The system comprised both a content management application and an augmented reality interface component for the creation of virtual exhibitions. The evaluation of ARCO not only assessed the final visitor experience, but also focused on operators and content developers, and was conducted via experimental set-ups and follow-up interviews. Evaluation showed that the system gave a good degree of customization and control; however, users had issues with setting different degrees of access privileges to contributors, and with the interfacing of the authoring system with content repositories (Sylaiou et al., 2008). As ARCO was not extensively evaluated in actual exhibition design practice beyond the original project, there is no empirical evidence of how it affected the work of curators and exhibition designers in the longer term.

The ARTECT toolkit (Koleva et al., 2009) was for the realisation of on-site interactive experiences, rather than fully virtual exhibitions, using mixed/augmented reality. Camera-based detection of markers could be configured to trigger images or 3D overlays on various devices, sound output, etc. The main principle for authoring was graphical linking of resources and rule-based execution of the resulting network. Many of the core insights learned from evaluation workshops with museum professionals are valid even for today's more complex tools. It was learned that authoring tools for domain experts need to be simple and to provide predictable ways of connecting physical and digital elements or resources, shielding the underlying software complexity from them. Museum experts wanted to take the physical arrangement of an exhibit and the envisioned visitor experience as starting point, and to explore scenarios and technical solutions from there. It was further found that supporting experimentation was important and that multiple levels of access for users with different (technical) expertise should be provided.

The CHESS Authoring Tool (CAT) supports the generation of personalised interactive experiences using mixed reality/augmented reality and pervasive games (Vayanou et al., 2014), and focuses on digital storytelling. Authoring follows a similar process as in moviemaking, from scripting, over staging, producing to editing, where stories are represented as graphs in the toolkit. The toolkit is for story authors to compose multimedia narratives, and is also used for delivery of the mixed reality narratives. CAT was evaluated in the CHESS project with staff from the two museums in the project. One of the challenging aspects of CAT that emerged from evaluation is grasping the idea behind the personalisation model and learning to compose stories on its basis—dividing the narrative into script units and developing several types of storylines. CAT is based on a commercial platform for authoring 3D content and AR experiences called Inscape (created by DIGINEXT), which is available as a commercial product but not specific to the heritage domain.

Another popular digital interaction frame for which toolkits have been developed is mobile multimedia tour guides. Weal et al. (2006) established requirements for authoring location-specific outdoor experiences. The project worked with teachers and curators in developing mobile-guided field trips in the gardens of Chawton House (UK). Insights from working with both user groups revealed a need for being able to author content on location (including definition of areas and points of interest while in-situ, note-taking, and situated recording of stories), combined with "desktop" editing and authoring to script, plan, prepare, and revise more complex sequences or tours. The focus on situated authoring was based on the observation that being on location often triggered ideas, which participants wanted to note immediately, enabled evaluation of ideas (appropriateness given the physical context), and that audio recordings made in-situ brought across the enthusiasm of curators, whereas off-site recordings felt stilted. Post-hoc editing should furthermore provide the opportunity to "relocate" content (i.e., associate it with another location). It was also envisioned that visitors might use the device to record questions, which could then drive and motivate authoring of new content. Cicero Designer enabled development of multi-device multimedia guides working across several (interconnected) platforms from mobile devices to stationary large screens (Ghiani et al., 2009). Curators could associate digital content, interactions, etc. to different places where interactive content should be delivered on devices. Features such as educational games could be added from a set of drag and drop available components. The toolkit was evaluated with a group of museum curators focusing mainly on its usability. Ardito et al. (2010) describe iterations of authoring tools for creating mobile interactive games to guide visits of school children at archaeological sites. One is *Explore!* (Ardito et al., 2012), which provides a framework for an educational game that can be adapted and populated with content by site staff. Staff can also easily update and change the experience for their audience.

A particular reason for needing bespoke guide toolkits are personalisation features and adaptivity to locations and visitor paths. A number of commercial products in this space exist. One example is the *Automatic Museum Guide* by Locatify,[28] which provides curators with templates and scripts for location-specific delivery of digital content so that they can create, update, and adjust mobile multimedia guides as they see fit.

An example of toolkit with great take-up is *Open Exhibits* (http://openexhibits.org/), which describes itself as a "free multitouch and HCI software initiative". It was funded by the U.S.'s National Science Foundation in 2010 and is run by IDEUM, an interactive design firm and multitouch surface producer. The project developed a multitouch, multi-user toolkit for creating interactive exhibits that are customized to a museum's needs. Applications are developed with a bespoke markup language (CML) in a software development kit, which includes a gesture analysis engine that not only supports multitouch but also other gesture technology (Kinect, LeapMotion). Museums across the world, and other informal learning institutions such as schools and libraries, share their know-how and templates on the Open Exhibits website. In 2014, Open Exhibits was linked with *Omeka*, an open-source web publishing platform for museums and libraries that supports digital online exhibitions (https://omeka.org/) (Kucsma et al., 2010). Unfortunately, while there are reports of museum projects on the openexhibits.org website, there are almost no academic publications associated with Open Exhibits.

The meSch toolkit (Figure 4.6) also focuses on tangible interactions, by means of authoring interactive experiences via a series of interconnected physical components (via an IoT setup) that can populate a physical exhibition or path through a heritage site. The toolkit comprises both software and hardware. The meSch *Authoring Tool* is an online platform to find inspiration (via a

28   https://locatify.com/automatic-museum-guide/.

"magazine" of "recipes": previously realised installations, that can be replicated or adapted), define interactive behaviour, manage content assets, and deploy the installation. The hardware consists of a set of tangible networked components, the meSch *IoT Kit*, with several sensors, NFC tags, and other IoT components used in various configurations to assemble an installation. The meSch toolkit was designed through a participatory approach with cultural heritage professionals (Not and Petrelli, 2019; Risseeuw et al., 2016). Core to the design of the user interface were the results of formative evaluation with heritage professionals. These indicated the need for a clear distinction between digital content and the physical context in which it will be delivered. This enables the reuse and repurposing of media content and hardware, as the same content can be deployed on different hardware configurations, e.g., detecting selection via button pressing, NFC readers, or proximity sensor. Conversely, the same context can hold different media, e.g., content in multiple languages. Users can use a recipe as template, customise the components that constitute it, their behaviour, and the associated digital content. A recipe can be modified as little or as much as desired: only replacing related content files, or modifying components and their behaviour, or adding new components. The toolkit is expandable by adding new hardware, however this requires knowledge of Javascript. Each level of customisation is represented by different tabs in the authoring tool interface. The meSch toolkit was evaluated also with users external to the project through a series of public workshops where participants realised tangible interactive installations from scratch. The workshops showed that the toolkit is usable and easy to understand. All groups were able to complete designs using the toolkit and all but one were able to realise a working prototype (Figure 4.7). However, it proved challenging to clearly communicate the tool's potential: the idea of tangible interaction was novel to participants, and for many not immediately graspable. Several people replicated interaction frames familiar to them (such as "standard" multimedia guides), and coaching and facilitation were needed to encourage them to re-think interactivity in different ways (as noted in Section 4.2, it can be challenging for heritage professionals to envision novel interaction frames and concepts). This shows how important a community of early adopters is in exchanging not only mutual support, but also ideas and examples that make a novel concept more familiar and understandable to others.

Creating toolkits gives non-technical users the opportunity of realising fairly advanced interactive experiences, rather than maintaining a separation between conceptual and technical design. However, a number of issues must be considered: designing a DIY platform is an ambitious undertaking—in terms of both technical development and design of the user interaction. It entails not only a vision of how to support use by a varied cohort of heritage staff, but also of the final outcomes a toolkit will generate and what additional support and resources it will provide. There is also an issue with the adoption of toolkits as they require take-up, familiarisation, and learning, and extensive practice to gain fluency. Museum staff and other cultural professionals might find them challenging, especially if the benefits of experimenting with a technology that might appear complex or obscure are not fully perceived and understood.

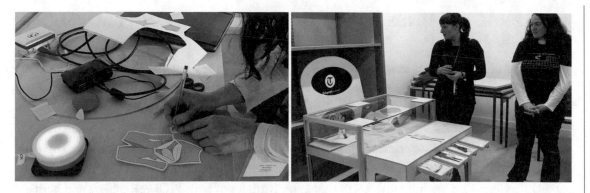

Figure 4.7: The meSch toolkit in use during a workshop with external participants. One group designed an augmented vanity table around historical fashion books, magazines, and souvenir underwear. Drawers representing different periods in British history contained maquettes of female clothes from those periods. Placing a maquette on the silhouette of a woman on top of the cabinet triggered video content about the life of women in that period. The group worked with the toolkit and lo-fi materials in the prototyping stage (left), and then demonstrated the completed functional installation into which components of the toolkit were embedded (right) (photographs by Luigina Ciolfi).

Just like any software platform, toolkits need long-term maintenance to remain accessible and functioning, and this might not be possible if the toolkit is the product of a project with a definite end. As we saw, a number of commercial toolkits are available and widely used. However, when it comes to more complex and advanced technology, toolkits are still mainly developed as part of research. Complex technologies are demanding to control, manage, and customise and might appear daunting to heritage professionals to handle even with the assistance of a toolkit and related support. For this reason, part of the research underpinning development of toolkits should also identify to what extent such technologies should be customisable by non-experts, and whether they can reasonably be adopted in museum practice in the long term. However, this is often not possible due to the limitation of funding schemes. If a toolkit is produced in other contexts (in industry, or by a community of enthusiasts), it is important to consider how this will be sustained and a full exploitation or business plan will be required. Furthermore, if a toolkit does become an established product and is used by a sizable number of people or institutions, it can be a challenge to keep track of all the times a DIY toolkit is downloaded, accessed, or used.

Having a community of practice that shares knowledge, stories of experiences, and best practice templates contributes greatly to the success of a toolkit. Gaining critical mass is another key issue, where substantial effort needs to be invested to create a community and to get users on-board. The role of word of mouth advertisement should not be underestimated in this respect. Therefore, efforts at running workshops at heritage conferences and fairs, as done by the Open Exhibits and the meSch project, are important strategies.

4.4   PRACTICAL ISSUES IN THE DESIGN AND DEVELOPMENT PROCESS

The choice of a model of design and development process for digital interactions in museums depends on several factors, and no approach is intrinsically preferable to others. For each instance, it is important to clarify the availability of the museum in terms of degree of support, participation, consultation, etc. A lot also depends on the goals of designing an interactive installation: for example, a main goal of experimenting with new technology will mean a very different approach in comparison to, for example, communicating a particular museum theme without much concern for technical novelty. Such priorities will shape the attitudes of both HCI researchers and heritage partners, and therefore the mutual agreement regarding how to establish partnership.

Approaching the design and development process, we must also consider the numerous practical points and constraints that influence prototyping and building of installations for museums: for example, robustness, maintenance, conservation, and greater curatorial aims. Installations need to run stable, as floor staff and technicians cannot be expected to reboot computers and restart software several times a day. The best solution is to automate a daily starting routine and shutdown that does not require any human attendance. To prevent systems from slowing down or stalling over the course of the day, it may even be useful to consider an automated restart every couple of hours (when the system is idle). If automated procedures are not possible, then adequate presence of researchers on the exhibit floor needs to be planned and resourced to provide assistance and support. Another practical issue to consider is that many museums do not power entire floors overnight, to reduce the risk of cable fire. In a past projects of ours, it was impossible for interactive devices to be recharged overnight for this reason.

Physical installations need to be very robust and withstand heavy use, in particular if young children are attending. When there are loose components, issues around replaceability need to be considered. How likely is it that visitors will remove components; can the system work without these; and what is the cost/ease of replacement? Sometimes, visitor behaviour is more careful than we anticipate, but this nevertheless needs consideration. In the context of one of the meSch exhibitions, an "emergency kit" was provided to museum staff to enable them to quickly make new tangible components should the original ones be damaged or lost.

If an installation involves authentic museum artefacts, their integrity is paramount from a conservation standpoint. It has to be ensured they are protected from damage and decay, so they are often secured behind glass. This influences what is feasible in terms of technology. In one of our projects, it was not possible to install a projector or other technology inside a glass showcase, as this would create heat and air flow, and would have made maintenance difficult (Pannier et al., 2016).

Maintenance also concerns the actual content and data as part of installations. Data and content management can be critical issues if a company owns the installation design, and thus all changes and updates have to be performed by them and paid for. Sometimes curators would like to update content because factual errors and mistakes are discovered. Sometimes the curatorial perspective may change, new artefacts are added to the collection and should then be integrated into digital systems, or it may be desired to take note of current events. Often museums lack access to the underlying database of digital installations, or do not have the technical knowledge or tools to edit and/or add content. This can even be the case if museum staff was part of an interdisciplinary design team, but the technology experts are not in-house. Furthermore, installations can also generate new content and data, for example by asking visitors to leave comments, create their own "storylines", or provide other feedback. As we discussed in Chapter 3, this also requires tools for management and upkeep.

CHAPTER 5

Evaluation in Museums

In the current chapter, we focus on evaluation studies of visitor behaviour and interaction in-situ, on the museum floor. On a strategic level, there is the distinction between front-end evaluation (done to gain insights informing exhibition planning, in particular on its audience), formative evaluation (done to improve prototypes in an iterative design process) and summative evaluation (evaluating completed projects). In Chapter 4, we already discussed formative evaluation approaches that inform ongoing design as part of an iterative, UCD. Here, we give an overview of the history of visitor studies (where it provides insights on conducting evaluations) and how the focus of analysis has diversified over time, and present the most important methodologies used for (summative) evaluation.

Figure 5.1: Evaluation methods and techniques include timing and tracking of visitors, audience questionnaires, and interviews with visitors (and staff), video observation of how visitors behave in the museum (with subsequent analysis), or the automated logging of interactions with digital installations (illustration by Katharina Bartholomäus).

The first studies of museum visitors were conducted in the 1920s and '30s. A diverse range of methods and methodologies for such studies have been utilised over time and continue to be used nowadays (see Hooper-Greenhill, 2006; Yalowitz and Bronnenkant, 2009). The dominant approach of a time period was often related to epistemological views of what visitors should do and "learn" in museums and what constitutes learning to start with (this was briefly summarized in Chapter 1).

Historically, visitor research started in the 1920s and '30s with approaches modelled on behavioural psychology, in particular measuring time spent by visitors and tracking their physical paths. This type of research became popular again in the 1970s and '80s with many studies on visitor orientation, circulation and wayfinding (Bitgood, 2006, 2011). In the 1960s, surveys focusing on visitor demographics became popular. However, these did not provide insight into *why* some people do not visit museums or visit them in a certain manner, and thus methods emphasizing subjectivity, such as interviews and focus groups, gained prominence. While open-ended questions and, for example, visitor-drawn sketches of their experience were used as early as the 1940s, methods for gaining insights on the visitors' subjective perspective only gained prominence once the "transmission-model of learning" (i.e., curators decide upon the content to be learned; studies evaluate such knowledge gain) slowly was replaced with a constructivist view of learning. If the visitor is viewed as "active audience" in "free-choice learning" (Falk et al., 2006; Falk and Dierking, 2000), then their experience becomes relevant and a variety of learning outcomes are valid, requiring a more open-ended exploration given that every person's experience will be different as their interests, motivations, and prior knowledge will differ.

From the 1990s onward, widely available video technology enabled detailed monitoring and analysis of visitor behaviour. This coincided with a "turn to understanding": that is, interpretative approaches that analyse how visitors construct meaning in interaction with the exhibits and each other. While these rely on gathering observational data, they differ from "tracking and tracing" approaches in the depth and scope of analysis and in the use of qualitative analysis approaches from ethnography, ethnomethodology and related areas.

Institutional approaches to evaluations often rely on post-visit data collection through surveys or questionnaires, and sometimes interviews. They further can include focus groups, which we will here subsume under interviews. These may cover specific exhibits (e.g., temporary flagship exhibitions) or the overall museum experience, including related facilities. Some of the methods that we describe in the following tend to be utilised primarily in academic research, because they require a more extensive set-up or can only be performed and analyzed by experts in the method, unlike simple tracking studies, questionnaires or structured interviews, which are easier to conduct and analyse, and for which temporary staff can be trained. Moreover, there is a tendency for "methodological conservatism" in institutional summative evaluation (Davies and Heath, 2014), in particular the fear that qualitative research methods might not provide generalizable findings.

All methods can suffer from limitations and biases that are familiar from HCI and other human subjects research: convenience-sampling for interviews and observation (or even tracking) may be non-representative; confirmation bias and demand characteristics influence responses in interviews or focus group as participants don't want to be too critical or aspire to be a "good participant"; mistakes in questionnaire design, etc. (Davies and Heath, 2014). Trialing and piloting of study protocols and tools are indispensable, determining feasibility, tweaking observation sheets, and question or interview guide design, testing logistics, and improving efficiency and effectiveness. As always, methods need to fit the research question(s), e.g., tracking studies will not reveal much on learning or empathy, and interviews do not reveal details of the steps by which visitors interact with installations. It is furthermore important to consider available resources in terms of collecting data and its analysis. Depending on the type of data collection, some work can be outsourced (to paid workers or volunteers). However, more complex methods require greater and more specialised expertise.

Evaluation approaches and setup should be communicated and negotiated upfront to the museum where one does a study to receive institutional approval and potentially logistical support, and to inform stakeholders and staff. Some museums might further have their own regulations regarding what kinds of data capture are permissible.

5.1   MIXED-METHOD VS. SINGLE-METHOD APPROACHES

It is usually recommended to utilise a mixed-method approach, as different methods gather information regarding different issues or across different time frames (i.e., observations of ongoing visit vs. post-visit survey to determine memorability). Moreover, different methods and types of data can complement or reinforce each other. This is called *triangulation*.

In our own work on the meSch project, when evaluating two exhibitions that trialled novel tangible interaction technologies (Damala et al., 2016), we combined questionnaires, semi-structured interviews, naturalistic observation, video observation and analysis, audio-recordings and log-files in one case, and in-person observation, visitor experience questionnaires, personal meaning maps, and interviews for the other exhibition. Choice of methods was related to the research questions, but also to the museum layout (which made video recording hard to implement in the second case), resources available, and on personal preferences for methods. The demand on project personnel was intensive, with 6–10 researchers involved (6 on-site, another 4 for data analysis) for the first case, and 2 on-site (and more for data analysis) for the second case. With such a complex and long evaluation, it is important to draw a detailed evaluation framework and plan, so that the overarching themes and questions that evaluation seeks to address are clearly mapped onto specific data collection activities and phases.

Nevertheless, evaluations can be conducted with fewer resources, although having less (diverse) data does restrict the kinds of analysis that are feasible. Hornecker and Stifter (2006a, 2006b) conducted interviews with visitors, open-ended observation in-situ, collected a photo documentary, and ran logfile analysis of installations to evaluate an exhibition at the Technical Museum in Vienna. Here, log-file data was central to convincing museum management that observational findings pointed to general issues, as well as confirming generalizability of some findings (when some exhibits were seen to be used only rarely over 16 hours of observation, the logfiles asserted that there were comparably few interactions over several months), and sometimes giving deeper insight into activity patterns. Qualitative methods were central to understanding underlying reasons and motivations.

Another example to do with scarce resources is the evaluation of *Reminisce* (Ciolfi and Mc-Loughlin, 2017): the visit took almost 2 hours and covered a large distance around the open air museum; evaluation had to be conducted by recruiting people specifically for the purpose of being studied (rather than capturing anyone going to the museum). Following visitors throughout the experience took a lot of time for a small team of researchers, and therefore the sample was small. However it covered the entire experience in detail. The shadowing of visitors was further complemented by an interview at the end of the experience.

One-person projects, as typical for Ph.D. work, may need to focus on one method of data collection and analysis, but can also benefit from diverse data sources. In a study at the Museum of Natural History in Berlin, Hornecker (2008, 2010) shadowed groups of visitors (who had volunteered) through the museum with video, did in-situ observation with extensive memoing and note-taking, a photo-documentary, and spent 1 hour counting visitors and coding their level of engagement with one prominent installation. Another example is the work of Claisse at The Bishops' House (Claisse et al., 2018) for which she designed two interactive installations taking the shape of physical, tangible artefacts such as cabinets, everyday objects from different time periods, and interactive tableaux. Evaluation was conducted by Claisse through naturalistic observation of visitors, and complemented by evaluation focus groups involving the volunteers running the museum, as the installations were inspired by and in turn affected their work. In order to maximise her opportunities for data collection, Claisse became a volunteer at the museum herself, an approach (also adopted by Maye et al., 2017) discussed in Chapter 4.

Evaluation can also focus on one expert method, as in the work of the Work, Interaction and Technology research group at King's College London (see Heath et al., 2002, Hindmarsh et al., 2005) who conduct ethnomethodological micro-analysis of video recordings, documenting instances of social, collaborative, and situated interaction around exhibits. Furthermore, a significant number of studies (e.g., Luke et al., 2007; Palmquist and Crowley, 2007) utilise video or audio-recording and code discourse, to assess interactional dynamics within groups of visitors or group learning.

5.2   METHODS AND TYPES OF STUDIES: TIMING AND TRACKING STUDIES

Yalowitz and Bronnenkant (2009) provide an overview of how timing and tracking methods have evolved, beginning with early studies that analysed wear patterns on carpets. Then, as a more principled approach, it became common for museums to hire and train short-time staff in the use of stopwatches and data sheets with predefined categories. Nowadays, where permissible, video can be used to document an exhibition (Damala et al., 2016), and the video could then be used at a later time to track visitors. It is important to note that this depends on both legal regulations regarding use of video, and the ability to place video cameras so they can record the entire exhibition. With the advent of mobile and ubiquitous technologies, visitor tracking has become amenable to automation (e.g., detecting and tracking visitor badges or guiding devices that keep their own log-files), and has thus risen in importance again. A problem of automated tracking is that it can rarely determine actual engagement (where are people looking, what are they talking about, etc.), albeit sophisticated arrangements, as described in Dim and Kuflik (2014), can detect where visitors are facing and mutual orientation within groups of visitors in terms of spatial proxemics.

Timing and tracking studies either focus on dwell time (or "holding power") of exhibits, or on tracking a visitor's path through an exhibition. Such studies can investigate, for example, the time spent within a defined area and the number of stops done for looking at exhibits, or the overall number of visitors stopping at exhibits. One well-cited study (Véron and Levasseur, 1983), found different patterns in how people explore exhibitions, analogizing these with animals, e.g., the ant (that systematically follows a path and observes almost all exhibits), the fish (exploring the entirety of a room without spending significant time at any exhibit), and so on. However, this study has been critiqued for inferring broad characteristics of visitors from simple behavioural traits, assuming that visitors deploy these attitudes consistently at every museum or exhibition and for linking these behaviours with prediction of interest and/or engagement (e.g., the "fish" being less engaged than the "ant", etc.).

Timing and tracking studies can also go in more detail (thus requiring a trained observer), coding, for instance, visitors' engagement form and level (looking at exhibits, inspecting, reading, non-exhibit related behaviour, etc.), as well as social interaction in-group/across group, and use of hands-on exhibits. Such studies can provide comparison data or inform placement of exhibits (e.g., placing new exhibits on a well-frequented path), or for re-planning the exhibit floor so as to "'lure" visitors into under-frequented areas. However these studies are limited in determining *why* visitors behave the way they do, or whether any learning takes place, and if so, what kind of learning. Moreover, the data from timing and tracking can be meaningless without considering the context (Yalowitz and Bronnenkant, 2009). For example, does it constitute success for a museum if 50% of visitors stop at 50% or more of exhibits? While this may be achievable (and indeed significant) for small museums, for a large museum this may be unrealistic as a goal, or simply not that informative as people could be fatigued, or might have visited before, or might be deeply interested only in certain exhibits. Indeed, if there are many repeat visitors, these will tend to focus on their favourite pieces only. An interesting example for a timing and tracking study is given by Pekarik et al. (2014) who combined timing-tracking data with questionnaire scores (regarding the types of experiences visitors are attracted to) to determine which kinds of exhibit setups (and accompanying poster and text) attracted different types of visitors at a museum of natural history.

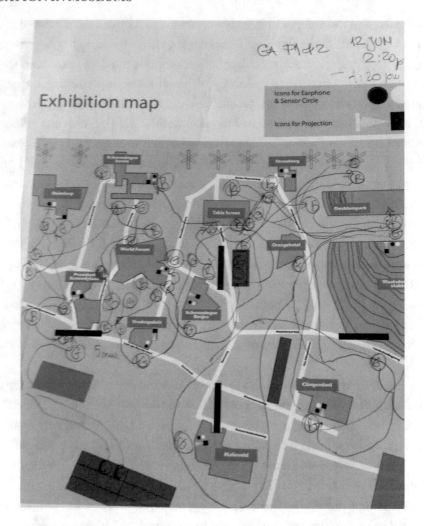

Figure 5.2: Timing and tracking studies often rely on bespoke aids to enable the researcher to better contextualise and refer to their data at a later stage. An example is using either existing or bespoke maps of the exhibition as a backdrop for each instance of the study. Researchers develop their own shorthand to represent individuals and their paths throughout an exhibit (photo courtesy of Gabriela Avram).

5.3 INTERACTION LOGS

Regarding interaction logs, we distinguish between tracking data (where exhibitions are augmented in ways that track visitors' locations) and interaction log-files from digital installations. With the latter, large amounts of data can be collected with relatively little effort, without much need for further instrumentation. Nonetheless, at software development stage it needs to be anticipated which data will be of interest and how to categorize it. In particular, for comparing different installations, standardisation is important. When Hornecker and Stifter (2006b) wanted to determine how often and for how long installations were used in a busy museum, it was essential to define what would count as an interaction session (i.e., interaction by one person or group). It was assumed that 2 minutes of inactivity meant that the original user had left and new users had taken over, defining activity after such a pause as a new interaction session. Being aware of such assumptions and definitions during data analysis is important—it would require visitor tracking to be sure that each interaction session relates to one visitor. Sometimes, in-situ observation resulted in questions that required adjustment of the software so to enhance log-file data. Log-files further revealed which elements of media content were most frequented, when visitors had a choice, as well as providing a general comparison of which installations were the most frequented and active (in non-idle mode) (see Figure 5.3).

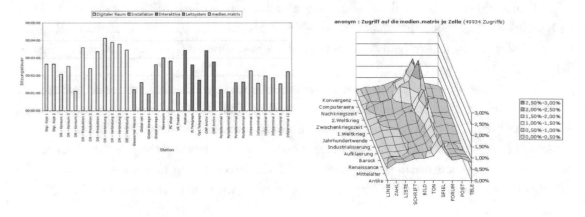

Figure 5.3: Examples of logfile data from the Technical Museum Vienna study. The left graph shows average session length at installations (i.e., how long people keep interacting). To interpret this, we also had to consider how many such sessions there were and the overall run-time of the installation (e.g., very few people might use an installation, but then stay long or many might use it for just a few seconds each). The right graph depicts which content was read most in the media-matrix (an information terminal with a matrix of content along eras and types of media) (Hornecker and Stifter, 2004).

The historical exhibition *The Hague and The Atlantic Wall*, designed for MUSEON (The Netherlands) as part of the meSch project, made use of replicas of actual museum objects: each replica (which embedded an NFC tag) corresponded to a different perspective on the exhibition, and triggered digital content related to that perspective at a number of interactive stations throughout the exhibition (Marshall et al., 2016; Not and Petrelli, 2019). This enabled access to extensive logs documenting usage by approximately 15,000 visitors over 7 months. These logs showed, for example, which object people chose most frequently, at which of the interactive stations people triggered content (and how frequently), for how long they remained, etc. Three of the replica objects were linked to content in Dutch and three in English. The logs showed that a majority of visitors chose Dutch. The logs were furthermore used to generate personalised data souvenirs based on each visitor's unique path of replica usage in the exhibition (Petrelli et al., 2017). They were used also for evaluation, although with the integration of data captured through other methods (such as questionnaires, interviews and naturalistic observations). For example, the logs showed that the most popular replicas (in both English and Dutch) were linked to the perspective of civilians affected by World War II (a tea bag and a sugar packet), however the logs on their own did not give any insights on whether this was due to the attractiveness of the object itself, or to the perspective represented. Through questionnaires and interviews, it was established that people's choice of replicas was overwhelmingly motivated by the perspective.

Other projects have used automated log-files as a source of evaluation data in combination with additional techniques for triangulation. Madsen and Madsen (2016) evaluated an AR installation reconstructing a 16th century chapel at Koldinghus Museum (Denmark), using logging and field observations.

Overall, log-files can provide important information in conducting evaluation, particularly giving insights on aggregate numbers of visitors and on finer details of interaction (e.g., timings, pauses, number of interaction instances) that are almost impossible to document thoroughly for an observer. However, they cannot provide the reasons why visitors behaved the way they did, nor rich data documenting their reactions and thoughts. For these reasons, log-files are usually analysed in conjunction with other related datasets in order to capture the visitor experience in full.

5.4   QUESTIONNAIRES

Questionnaires belong to the standard repertoire of methods for HCI and museum studies. Demographic information, the motivation for a visit and visitor satisfaction, can be collected in a low-cost and structured way. The widespread use of survey questionnaires by museums is often related to their need to justify funding or document their performance, and produce reports to public funding or governing bodies (see Davies and Heath, 2014). Museums want and need this kind of data (visitor numbers, satisfaction ratings, demographics) and are often concerned that academic evaluations do not provide them. Some museums might not be aware that other kinds of evaluations exist and/or may be wary of their value. For negotiating access and partnership, it can thus be a door-opener for researchers to offer help in gathering such kind of data that is useful to the museum.

When there are limited resources for doing research on-site and when responses from large numbers of visitors are sought, questionnaires can be useful. They can be handed out by museum staff, for instance at the ticket counter, or by paid helpers, as commonly used by museums for evaluations of visitor satisfaction and demographics, given that little training is required for such tasks.

Questionnaires can also be useful to investigate visitors' attitudes toward digital innovations that are at proposal stage or in the early stages of development, and not yet warrant more time-consuming methods for data collection. An example is the study by Pitsch et al. (2011) on the attitudes of German museum visitors toward robotic guides. Wilson et al. (2018) investigated what factors visitors find important in 3D-printed replicas, using a guided questionnaire approach (where a researcher assists). Participants first handled different replicas and then completed semantic differential scales, which were based on descriptions elicited from a prior interviewing study with another set of replicas. Participants then rated replicas and provided a rationale for their preferences.

Questionnaires in museums suffer the known issues from the literature on research methods, in particular self-selection of respondents, when these are simply put out to answer. Experience shows that online questionnaires or surveys post-visit are rarely filled out, and even paper questionnaires may be put aside by many visitors. Some museums experiment with questionnaires on touchscreens within the museum. But, similar to online questionnaires, this approach suffers from self-selection, response rates are unknown; moreover, the risk is that only a fraction of visitors completes these. The touchscreen questionnaire is in competition with surrounding exhibits as any other object in the museum, and probably much less interesting. The most effective method remains having someone there in person who approaches visitors and hands out paper questionnaires, ideally to have them answered immediately, or to approach those that exit the museum to ask them to return their questionnaires.

Questionnaires are a limited way of collecting data, given that they are meant to be filled by visitors on their own, without the assistance and coaching of a researcher, and within a short timeframe. Therefore, they need to be well thought out. Besides demographic information, questionnaires can include rating and comparing installations, exhibits, or objects, simple indicators of personal interest and motivation to visit, and some open questions regarding what visitors might appreciate on a return visit. Despite these limitations, questionnaires are a useful way to get research data, and they are very established in the museum world, which can positively influence the museum's willingness to support administering them as part of research projects. Mylonakis and Kendristakis (2006) provide a useful overview of indicators that museums are keen to collect when evaluating their service with visitors via questionnaires, and it can be useful to HCI researchers to plan questionnaire studies in partnership with museums. Museums themselves (particularly public ones) also often make reports available that analyse the results of questionnaire studies of visitor satisfaction, and this can be important material to help researchers plan evaluations.

5.5   INTERVIEWS

Interviews have historically been one of the most prominent methods in museum research, in particular for research investigating visitor motivation (e.g., Pekarik et al., 1999). They are a common way to evaluate entire exhibitions and to gain insight into what is memorable for visitors, their motivations, and impressions. Interviews thus provide complementary information to observational methods and give deeper, richer insights than questionnaires. In particular, interviews can be conducted both short- and long-term post-visit, enquiring into direct impressions and opinions, the rationale for behaviours during the visit, and to determine longitudinal influences and recollection or learning gains of the visit (see, e.g., Bamberger and Tali, 2008).

Post-visit interviews with visitors leaving an exhibition (Hornecker and Stifter, 2006a) revealed unexpected reasons for why some visitors chose not to use touchscreen information stations, with some visitors stating that they use computers in their everyday work and wanted a break. Most visitors preferred to drift through the museum, rather than using the digital guide system made available. Interview data thus revealed the underlying reasons for phenomena from the interaction logs, where the interaction logs demonstrated that said phenomena and behaviours were persistent and common. Weilenmann et al. (2013) investigated the use of Instagram in museums by studying publicly available Instagram photos from a natural history museum as well as recruiting 16 instagrammers to post Instagram photos of their museum visit, and interviewing them to gain insight into the choices underlying their creations. As part of a multi-method strategy, Kollmann (2007) conducted exit-interviews with randomly selected visitors leaving museum galleries, asking them about "broken exhibits" encountered and their levels of disappointment. This provided insights into *when* visitors perceive an exhibit as "broken", which sometimes was related to lacking functionality or to usability issues.

As always, interviews should be well prepared in terms of question design and pilot-tested. Post-visit interviews are especially useful in combination with prior observation, when visitors can be asked why they behaved in a certain way. This requires skill and tact, as visitors should not feel they have been followed around all the time. Willingness to take part in an interview can be increased if interviewees are rewarded with a small gift or at least a drink in the museum cafeteria. After the visit, many people are tired, and either want to sit down and relax or go home, thus interviews in the cafeteria are often appreciated. Finding participants for longitudinal studies can be difficult, as these need to be recruited directly after (or before) a visit, contact details need to be collected, and a date for the interview needs to be scheduled. Interviews can have different degrees of structure: from highly structured interview guides to open-ended interviews. Due to the time and resource constraints of conducting evaluations in museums and the need to put limited pressure on visitors who may be tired, structured, and semi-structured interviews are usually employed in these settings. A semi-structured approach is very often used as the interview guide allows for some degree of digression and deeper probing in combination with more focused questions. The additional probing can be cut short or avoided if the interviewees show signs of fatigue. Furthermore, it can be helpful if the interviewer clearly is a third party to the institution (and to the exhibit development), as visitors tend to be reluctant to criticise (Davies and Heath, 2014).

Interviews are usually transcribed, and then analysed. Depending on analysis approach, this may mean transcribing the words spoken (also called "intelligent verbatim" transcription), or to also transcribe pauses, emphasis, and other speech patterns (verbatim transcription). There is a range of approaches from the social sciences for how to analyze interviews. The most commonly used ones for visitor studies and most accessible rely on coding approaches to identify patterns and themes (for instance, thematic analysis; Braun and Clarke, 2006). Coding can be theory-led, identifying categories that are derived from existing theory, or can be bottom-up, inductively, with categories emerging from the data ("grounded"). As these approaches also apply for observational methods and video analysis, these will also briefly be discussed in the following sections.

5.6   OBSERVATIONAL METHODS

Observation is essential to investigate actual conduct of visitors, which may sometimes critically differ from what people report in interviews. Observation is also crucial to capture how visitor conduct links to the context where it occurs. Observational methods can follow a structured approach (coding and tracking) or a more naturalistic, open-ended and "grounded" approach aimed at capturing emergent insights. A specific type of observational approaches concerns ethnographic studies, which usually combine interviewing and observation with deep immersion into the context. One could argue that it is not actually possible to do a proper ethnography of museum visitors, since ethnography requires longer-term immersion in a culture and participation in its practices, whereas museum visitors do not really form a persistent "community of practice". It is, however, possible to conduct ethnographies of museums as institutions, if deemed relevant to the specific project. Nevertheless, ethnographic methods can inform qualitative observational studies of visitors, in particular if these combine interviewing, shadowing of visitors along a visit and extended in-situ observation.

Unlike with interviews or questionnaires, the researcher normally does not directly approach potential participants, so there are ethical issues around informed consent. While the details need to be agreed upon in each case, a standard procedure for this is to have signs at the entry to the museum and around those areas under focused observation, informing people about the research taking place: "Visitor Observation Study: Today an observational visitor study is taking place in the museum for reasons of research and evaluation. We are <institution>, studying <insert rough aims>. For this, a researcher will be present and observe in some areas. <add other methods used>. Please contact <names and details> if you have any concerns" (example of phrasing). Researchers would also normally wear identification badges.

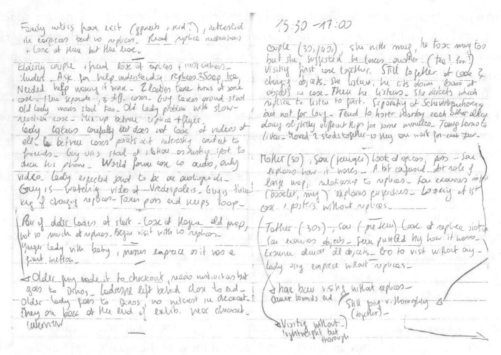

Figure 5.4: Sample page from observational notes. Researchers develop their own strategies for taking notes during open-ended observation sessions, such as ways to identify people being observed and to mark notable occurrences that have happened (photograph by Luigina Ciolfi).

A particular approach sometimes used in heritage settings is shadowing. Rather than focusing observation on a particular installation, or unique point of the visit, and capturing the interactions of various users, shadowing entails focusing on one visitor or visiting unit (such as a family group) and moving with them as they go through the exhibition. Shadowing may entail following visitors either at some distance (for example to note where they have stopped and for how long), or actually joining a group, as a "legitimate peripheral participant". Consent should always be sought. Shadowing is an effective method to capture evaluation data when the interaction is not confined to a standalone installation, is distributed across various locations, or involves a mobile component that may be used in-between points. Capturing this physical and interactional flow is essential in this case to understand the full visitor experience. Issues to consider when using shadowing are the fairly high degree of obtrusiveness (particularly in smaller museums, where spaces might be more confined), and its time-consuming nature (it can take several hours to capture one instance of visitor experience). An example is the evaluation of the *Reminisce* installation at Bunratty Folk Park (Ciolfi and McLoughlin, 2017), where 23 visiting units who agreed to participate were observed as they interacted with the entirety of the installation at seven different sites in the large Park. Despite the small number of participants (for the reasons mentioned earlier), the data collected was very rich and enabled the researchers to evaluate several aspects of the installation, from the use of tangible components (Ciolfi and McLoughlin, 2011), to the evocative and emotional aspects of the visit (Ciolfi and McLoughlin, 2012). Hornecker (2010) also used shadowing techniques, joining five visitor groups that had volunteered for this, as well as doing observation focused on two installations. Shadowing a group's entire visit gave some insight into whether behaviour at the installations was typical for this group, and allowed the researcher to listen in to conversations in a more natural way, as over time, her presence in the group became more 'normal' and her role became more that of a legitimate participant.

Given the limitations of human memory, in open-ended observation it is central to engage in extensive note-taking (see Figure 5.4), borrowing from ethnographic practices. Notes can relate to anything observed, from sketches of visitor configurations around exhibits, descriptions of behaviours, snippets of conversations overheard, to summaries of insights and emerging hypotheses. Descriptive note-taking (reporting facts) needs to be distinguishable from reflection, interpretation, and conclusions, which are also jotted down as they occur. Some researchers also use audio notes and (when permitted by the ethics framework of the research) photographs to complement notes. Observation can utilise tactics of sampling and triangulation. For example, one can alternate between observing one exhibit and following groups over a larger trajectory, one can pick visitors randomly (every 10th that enters the room), or based on strategic sampling (how do older visitors behave compared to teenagers).

Data analysis can then be guided by thematic analysis and other approaches to grounded analysis, when following an open-ended, qualitative approach. Structured coding approaches, on the other hand, require clear categories to code for, often based on theoretical foundations (e.g., existing models for measuring conversations' level of learning-related talk). These are thus related to complex timing and tracking approaches (which might track and measure a number of activities that visitors do, such as looking at objects, reading text, reading instructions, discussing, wayfinding, etc). With structured coding, pre-determined categories are also used in on-site note-taking. Choice of categories (and the theoretical foundations that determine categories) should be explicit and well considered.

5.7   VIDEO OBSERVATION AND ANALYSIS

Despite the richness of detail it can reveal on how visitors exactly behave face to face with exhibits, video observation and analysis is still not utilised much in institutional research, with few exceptions (Humphrey et al., 2005), and is mostly popular in academic research (Davies and Heath, 2014). Video allows for precise, fairly unobtrusive data collection, as well as detailed and repeated viewing that can give fine-grained insights into visitor interactions (vom Lehn et al., 2002). Moreover, the same set of data can be analyzed repeatedly, using different approaches or focusing on different aspects. Yet video analysis can be extremely time-consuming, and it is easy to collect far more data than can ever be investigated. Analysis methods range from ethnomethodological micro-analysis of how interaction unfolds (Heath et al., 2010), other forms of micro-analysis such as conversation analysis, to coding approaches, either based on emergent categories or on pre-defined schemes (similar as with observational approaches). Note that it is imperative to ascertain whether video-recording is permitted by local legal regulations, as audiovisual recordings are sometimes covered by CCTV regulations or, e.g., the new EU privacy regulations.

Figure 5.5: For large installations, setting up cameras can turn complex. The GlenDouglas steam train installation at the Riverside Transport Museum in Glasgow is approx. 5 meters long and has three control sections (Clarke and Hornecker, 2013). The left photo shows a frontal view from a distance. A camera placed on the left display case (white arrow) provides the view in the middle photo, focusing on people at the first control section. The right-hand view is captured by a camera placed on the green wall facing the installation (white arrow). Note that only half of the installation and setup is shown above: a third camera was used to record activity at another control panel toward the right and a fourth for the view from the far right. In addition, audio recorders were hidden at control panels. For analysis, video from four cameras and two separate audio-tracks had to be synched and merged (photographs by Eva Hornecker).

Many decisions need to be made at study design stage (see Heath et al., 2010), including on camera placement, angle, distance from exhibits, the duration of study and role of researchers (e.g., whether to completely rely on recording or whether to be present for part of the time). Sometimes, options might be constrained by the study setting or health and safety concerns (for example, number of locations that are safe to set-up a camera, or accessible power outlets for charging), and there needs be careful planning and support by museum managers. A challenge regarding the use of video are ethical concerns and legal regulations, which vary between countries and change over time (see the new EU regulations on privacy). Unfortunately, being aware of observation changes people's behaviour, and having a camera installed in a gallery space can stand out (especially in spaces where photography and filming are not allowed), reminding visitors of being under observation. Block et al. (2015) found that consent procedures can alter patterns of engagement, even if this just means entering an area cordoned off for videotaping. Overall, it is indispensable to clarify regulations up-front and to receive approval from the relevant authorities and ethics monitoring bodies, which is best done in collaboration with the museum itself.

Figure 5.6: It is sometimes possible to take advantage of the infrastructure of the exhibition gallery to place cameras, for example using built-in rigs that house light fittings and other equipment (projectors, screens, etc.). This needs the museum management's permission and support in terms of health, safety, and security, and requires planning of how to control video recording and how often, which angle to capture, etc. One advantage of this approach is that the cameras will be less obtrusive compared to placing them at floor level in the exhibition (photo courtesy of Gabriela Avram).

The type of analysis method used can impact on the amount of data that is needed. For qualitative micro-analysis, given the material will be analysed in extreme detail, it can be enough to have a few hours of data. For more quantitative style coding approaches, it is important to have representative amounts and types of data, which requires recording at least over several days. Logistical issues also need to be resolved. For one study (Damala et al., 2016), the small size of rooms made it impossible to position cameras adequately, and there were no power outlets available, thus making video recording impractical.

Video or audio recordings can, for example, be analyzed for patterns of conversation around exhibits, identifying, for instance, whether these trigger patterns related to scientific enquiry, result in cross-generational discourse, and what roles emerge in families (see, for example, Palmquist and Crowley's (2007) work on how parents and children talk about dinosaurs, and Ciolfi and McLoughlin's (2017) discussion of intergenerational conversations at Bunratty Folk Park), or to compare activity and participation patterns across different versions of an exhibit (Horn et al., 2009) compare a screen-based and a tangible puzzle version for programming a robot, where the tangible version resulted in children being more active and more girls being active). In our evaluation of the *Atlantic Wall* exhibition at MUSEON (Marshall et al., 2016), audio and video recordings at the station where visitors chose a replica object representing different perspectives revealed that choosing a replica was a highly social process, both the replicas and the perspectives being discussed and negotiated within groups.

Coding can be based on predetermined categories that are frequently informed by more theoretical work, or on emergent codes, where recurrent patterns are identified in repeated viewings of the data. Such patterns are described and named, and the data then is systematically coded along these (note that this also applies for analysis of interviews or observational data). Hornecker and Nicol (2012) coded video of family interactions around interactive museum installations using categories informed by literature on parent-child interaction. This revealed differences in how much parents scaffolded children's interactions at different installations and how much educational talk occurred (giving contextual information, relating to general phenomena and abstract concepts or to other artefacts in an exhibition. etc.). It also showed that family behaviours during prototype evaluation sessions differed markedly from that of families observed "in-the-wild".

Micro-analysis of video (for an introduction into the method see Heath, Hindmarsh, and Luff, 2010) is exemplified by the work from Christian Heath and Paul Luff (Heath and Luff, 2000) and their colleagues, who analyzed human coordination practices in as varied domains as control rooms, trading rooms, and museums. In this style of analysis, both verbal and non-verbal behaviours are considered in their role in human communication and coordination, and the focus lies on analyzing the sequential unfolding of interaction, where people react to each other's actions (and that of devices or technologies). In particular, their work with vom Lehn revealed how visitors in galleries and museums coordinate and often are influenced by the behaviours of strangers and/or onlookers in the same space. It highlighted the role of visitors' bodily behaviour (posture and gesturing) in discriminating objects, negotiating what to look at and talk about (Heath and vom Lehn, 2004) and how such bodily behaviour does "animate exhibits, highlight particular elements and dramatize certain features" (Heath et al. 2002; Heath and vom Lehn, 2004; vom Lehn et al., 2007).

Micro-analysis can also reveal instances where installations fail to support group interaction. For instance, in a comparison of two versions of the *Jurascope* installation (Hornecker, 2010), where one showed location-specific animations through a big telescope-type device and the other provided the same animations on a public screen, dialogue around the public screen resembled a conversation pattern. In contrast, when individual visitors looking through the telescopes commented on what they (but only them!) saw, this was often met with silence or ignored by the rest of the group; even if another person attempted a reply, the conversation fragmented. Micro-analysis further revealed how visitors frequently "indexed" between the animations and the exhibits close-by that the animations directly related to (pointing back and forth, discussing how the two relate to each other), and how the spatial organisation and careful alignment of lines of sight contributed to this (Hornecker, 2016). Best (2012) combined micro-analysis and conversation analysis of video recordings from guided tours in a historic house with ethnographic style fieldwork and learning to guide house tours herself in an analysis of the nature of guided tours. This analysis highlighted how guides interact with visitors, adapting their behaviour, guiding attention, reacting to visitors, rather than following a scripted monologue.

5.8   CONTENT ANALYSIS

For installations or other settings that result in datasets of user-generated content, methods for content analysis can be utilised for evaluation. The data collection could be interpreted as a form of "logging" (discussed already), but analysis methods differ from that of interaction log-files, that typically are investigated with statistical methods. Content analysis usually borrows from approaches used in other disciplines and the approaches already discussed, such as open coding, coding along given themes, or forms of micro-analysis. Weilenmann et al. (2013) analyzed Instagram photos from a museum, categorizing them by what was shown in the photos, how they were manipulated, and captions and hashtags added. Moreover, they took into account how ordering of photos in a user's Instagram feed created a narrative of the museum visit. Patel et al. (2015) in a study of an installation that invited visitors to provide fictional dictionary entries, found that this resulted in different types of entries, from redefining and recharacterizing existing words, transforming names into verbs, creating new words or generating a verb from a noun, generating compound words or homophones.

5.9   ASSESSING LEARNING

Assessing visitor learning in museums is tricky because it depends on so many factors. We discussed earlier that museum learning is "free-choice learning" (Falk and Dierking, 1992, 2013) and will depend on visitors' prior experiences, knowledge, and interests. Moreover, an exhibition may motivate visitors to learn more about a topic, but this then happens later, outside the museum. Some exhibitions even have the goal of creating empathy and interest (instead of direct learning)—museum experiences are varied and include imaginative engagement, experience of beauty, or encountering rare objects (Pekarik et al., 1999). The outcome of such experiences may involve increasing understanding, creating meaning, or may influence attitudes and resulting actions (e.g., becoming more environmentally-conscious), or visitor self-perception and identity, and development of skills (Perry,

2012). Research methods that attempt to assess visitor learning should thus take account of individuals' learning agendas (which may furthermore change over time), the broad range of learning outcomes (skills, values, awareness, knowledge, etc.), and should address longer-term learning and attitude changes.

A comparative study by Sanford (2010), simultaneously gathering data on time spent at an exhibit for families, level of exhibit engagement (coded as: looking at, manipulating individual parts, and coordinating several elements of the exhibit) and interpretative talk (describing the exhibit, analyzing it, explaining), revealed that there was little relation between the three measures, suggesting that we cannot rely on only one measure to assess learning. For instance, exhibits which are low on some measures might nevertheless foster learning (e.g., a short, but complex conversation triggered by a short interaction).

The San Francisco Exploratorium has long conducted research projects on how to improve people's engagement with science, and contributed some of the most extensive work on visitor learning, developing a detailed evaluation approach. Its aim is to encourage "*active prolonged engagement (APE)*": that is, meaningful interaction that generates personally and socially constructed knowledge via open-ended visitor-initiated play and experimentation (Humphries et al., 2005). The Exploratorium develops its exhibits in-house[29] and often puts early versions on the floor for testing, using video recording and observations to identify whether an exhibit generates APE-style discussion and works well.

An APE-redesign process was conducted for exhibits that require different types of visitor interaction: from actively exploring phenomena, to more systematic investigation of the laws of physics in playful exhibits, to pure observation (watching water freeze), and construction tasks. Exhibits are video recorded and visitor interactions are then coded along various categories. Besides overall holding time (time spent), the video is coded for specific behaviours, both verbal and nonverbal. This can include: the number and type of experiments done, the types of questions people in a group ask each other (ask for manipulation, for explanation, for guidance, for others' perception or opinion, or off-topic questions), the responses given (reading something, use or discuss, ignoring of question, or off-task), as well as the reasons for leaving an exhibit. Another (of various) coding categories related to learning is the critical thinking skills checklist (Luke et al.,2007), which includes physical participation, interpretive questions/explanations, teamwork, evaluations, and comparisons made or the Scoring Qualitative Informal Learning Dialogue (SQuILD) method for quantifying idiosyncratic social learning talk (Roberts and Lyons, 2017). The underlying rationale for these approaches (informed by work on science education and collaborative learning) is that learners' dialogue mirrors the patterns of scientific inquiry, with hypotheses stated and questions asked, and experiments set up to test or answer the former. In particular for children visitors, conversation

---

[29] At the San Francisco Exploratorium, some of the workshops where interactive exhibitions are created are actually in full sight of visitors, hence becoming part of the exhibit floor.

improves remembering, supports learning, and, in general, conversation enforces joint construction of meaning (Perry, 2012).

One of the outcomes of the APE project was a change of policy in exhibit signage and labeling (as well as poster design) to encourage open-ended exploration and hypotheses-making-and-testing, rather than pushing visitors to answer a given question and read given explanations, since the latter resulted in shorter, less rich interactions. Moreover, it was realized that exhibits with rich, varied outcomes can nevertheless be easily accessible and reliably trigger initial engagement, if there is many reliable entry points that all trigger interesting responses from the exhibit. The project further highlighted the importance of clear, active exhibit titles that make it evident how to interact, using open questions instead of mere instructions.

Personal Meaning Mapping (PMM) was developed by John Falk and colleagues (1998) to assess how visitors' understanding of a topic has changed due to a visit. Participants either draw something similar to a mind-map or just write words and phrases associated with a topic on a paper, first before the visit (pre-visit map) and then afterward (often several months later), adding written explanations. The PMM is often accompanied by a semi-structured interview for more insights. These maps can then be compared along four dimensions of learning: the *extent* of visitors' knowledge (the size of the vocabulary used); *breadth* (number of concepts used); *depth* (the richness of how these concepts are described); and *mastery* (identifying the visitor's understanding as novice or expert). PMM allows for identification of diverse learning outcomes and is fairly easy to conduct in terms of raw data collection, but requires some expertise for analysis as well as knowledge of the actual subject matter in order to rate depth and level of knowledge. In the meSch project, the PMM was used to compare people's understanding of objects accompanied by text labels with that of objects accompanied by digital components, in a museum of antique art. Visitors thus received two PMM sheets, with the photo of an object in the middle, to annotate. To distinguish pre-visit and post-visit answers, they were given different colored pens.

5.10   EVALUATION IN INSTITUTIONAL PRACTICE

In the above sections, we focused on evaluation approaches used in academic research. In closing this chapter, we provide some additional pointers to how practitioners from heritage and visitor studies traditions and from museums do evaluations.

Nelson and Cohn (2015) provide an overview of data collection methods used by museums for evaluations, particularly for assessing learning. Their overview resonates with the one we have given in this chapter, however with the additional discussion about how to set goals for the evaluation of whether learning was achieved. The UK visitor studies group has an "evaluation toolkit for museum practitioners" available online[30], which provides a summary of types of evaluations and

---

[30]   http://visitors.org.uk/wp-content/uploads/2014/08/ShareSE_Evaltoolkit.pdf.

their aims and benefits for museums, and a basic introduction into the relevant techniques, with step by step guidance, as well as UK-specific data protection issues. A similar comprehensive *Practical Evaluation Guide* for museums is provided by Diamond et al. (2016), with a focus on evaluating informal learning.

Lynda Kelly has been documenting the work of the Australian Museum Audience Research Centre (AMARC) for decades. She provides an overview of the development of audience research over time and describes several case studies from AMARC of front-end, formative, and summative evaluation (Kelly, 2004). This article further discusses the relation between exhibition evaluation and research, arguing that museums should move toward using evaluations as a chance for organisational learning and change, with a research mindset that does not just evaluate a specific exhibition, but aims to increase understanding of visitor experience, learning, behaviour, etc.

In a meta-study that was motivated by the apparent lack of impact of summative evaluation studies in museums and galleries, Davies and Heath (2014) investigated the reasons for this and derived a set of recommendations. One issue is that it can be difficult to draw more general conclusions from studies or to compare several studies, when each uses a different set of approaches for data collection, and for data analysis. From an institutional standpoint, it can thus be desirable to develop a consistent approach to evaluation. Further, it appears that summative evaluation is rarely seen as an opportunity for reflection and learning, especially given that at the time it takes place, there is usually no funding remaining and the exhibition team has been disbanded—evaluations thus rarely result in changes and re-design of exhibitions. "Political" and structural challenges can further prevent discussion and sharing of findings between organisations. They recommend that evaluation should have a higher strategic value for museums, to plan to share evaluation findings and support comparison and synthesis from studies, to devise overarching research questions that studies then address, and to broaden the range of methods.

CHAPTER 6

Conclusions

Museums are going through systematic change: in the way they operate and as bodies interfacing with publics, other institutions, and with society in general. From places devoted to heritage preservation and education, they are increasingly becoming places for community engagement, dialogue and even questioning around political or societal issues. However, the risk is that a rhetoric of social action or community empowerment is used by museums without truly being embedded in their missions and ways of working. In Elaine Heumann Gurian's words: "*this can lead to a facile expression that is often unexamined and, at its worst, might be termed expedient and even cynical*" (Heumann Gurian, 2006, p. 49). According to Heumann Gurian, museums should (while maintaining an overarching commitment to public service) narrow their direction and specialise in particular ways of engaging the public with heritage. She identifies five categories of museum "missions": object-centred museums, where the priority is the preservation of artefacts and the identity is that of "*temples of the contemplative*"; client-centred museums, focusing rather on the type of audience than on the content (e.g., children's museums); community-centred museums, whose primary concern is the engagement and well-being of the communities that they represent (e.g., religious or ethnic minorities, geographically defined communities, professional communities, etc.) often taking on the role of forums for these communities; national (and government) museums, representing national history, identity, and character (Heumann Gurian, 2006). While it is possible for a museum to embrace more than one of these overall approaches, it has to be done with care and consideration. This, of course, has implications on how digital technologies are utilised, and on how visitors can be engaged through them. Choosing specific approaches to designing technologies, ways of delivering interaction opportunities, and ways to evaluate and reflect on impact must be done with due consideration.

People's evolving relationship with digital technologies also plays a role: museums were for a long time places where new technologies brought in a "wow factor". This is more difficult to achieve now as people have many experiences with advanced technology in their lives. The increasing culture of "digital sharing" by people (via social media, etc.), is also more and more pervasive in the context of heritage visits, and might shape the approaches to and impact of interpretation strategies: independently of whether museums offer digital tools and experiences themselves, these will cross the museum doors and be part of how audiences conduct their visit.

At the same time, "the digital" is more than ever deeply entwined with museum practices, from preservation, to interpretation and communication (Parry, 2013). Samis (2018) argues that while, in the early days of digital museum technologies, those people and museums who did embrace them could truly experiment and even subvert the traditional traits of museums, now such pervasiveness has meant the institutionalisation of the digital, and correspondingly a more conservative approach to what it does for museums and their audiences, missing out opportunities and possibly putting too much faith onto technology alone as a solution to wide engagement. However, despite being embedded into museum strategies, the uptake of digital tools in museums (guides, etc.) remains limited to a minority of visitors. Samis advocates a "blended" approach, where human intervention, physical exhibits and spaces, and digital technology work together.

From the perspective of HCI, current trends and interests can also affect how museums and their audiences are impacted and how the practice and scholarship within the field evolves.

Museums have been ground for experimentation of new and emerging technologies (from the early days of VR and AR, to more recent explorations of computer vision and machine learning), sometimes at the cost of effectiveness in terms of fit with the museum's remit and in terms of visitor experience. This is a tension (and an unresolved one) in the HCI body of work in and for museums: is it positive and useful to experiment with technology in museums as they are safe and relatively risk-free public places even if the technology might not be well fitted to the context? Or should we treat museums with a more cautious attitude?

These of course are open questions that cannot be answered univocally, and depend on many other factors such as type of project and partnership with museums, intended goals, etc. However, they must be taken into account when embarking in projects in collaboration with heritage institutions.

What have we learned from our own experience?

From some of our observations over the years, it has often been the simpler installations, with less complex (but one could also argue: tightly focused) functionality, that appeared to be more effective in eliciting strong visitor engagement and meaningful discussion amongst groups. It can be tempting to use the powers of digital technologies in order to give access to vast amounts of information, to develop sophisticated interaction scenarios, or to incorporate brand-new technologies. But this does not always result in successful exhibits (and, if done as an intentional experiment, UCD should be properly evaluated in order to inform future design). Especially with novel technologies, it can often take some time and experimentation to determine how to put it to best use, as for example evidenced with initial first applications of multi-touch screens.

Museums are places attracting multiple categories of people (in terms of age, provenance, gender, motivation to visit, etc.) and of practices (leisure, education, socialising, community building, etc.). General-purpose interactive technology might thus not be as successful as it is hoped, and a degree of bespokeness (i.e., technology that is tailored for a certain subgroup, or focused to support a certain activity) could be more effective.

We believe that it is important to think about how digital installations and the (physical) museum space interact and complement each other, and what kinds of interactions and activities they engender for visitors—interactions and activities that have visitors engage with the contents, objects, and concepts of the museum—and not with the technology for its own sake. Having a sound understanding of the physical, social, and cultural context of museum visiting, and of typical behaviours and motivations of visitors, helps to assess design concepts for potential pitfalls and to know where to put the focus on in user testing and evaluation. Moreover, in working with and in museums, it can be invaluable to have an understanding of the museum as organisation and professional work context. In this respect, establishing and maintaining an effective partnership with museums is of key importance.

From the point of view of process, we believe that there is no universal approach to guarantee success. It is wise not to assume that one development model, or interaction frame, or methodological approach works everywhere. As we have seen, museums are incredibly varied in terms of typologies, organisational models and target audiences, and the way to approach the design and evaluation of interactive technologies needs to be tailored to them.

A more traditional UCD approach can be effective to produce successful designs, however it might not concern itself with long-term impact beyond the life of a (research) design project, where museum staff no longer have access to the resources and expertise to maintain installations that are often experimental in nature. Participatory Design (co-design) has been increasingly popular. Evaluation has shown that it can lead to greater long-term impact on the museum (its strategy and its staff, also in terms of skills), but not necessarily to great novelty of the HCI research, as shared decision making might lead to choosing or developing technological platforms that are less innovative in terms of functionality, but more robust and manageable.

For all these reasons, it is important to clarify priorities in terms of advancing the HCI state of the art versus aiming for long-term impact and extended empirical evaluation.

Overall, the legacy of HCI projects in museums is always a difficult and sensitive issue to handle: it can lead to further successful experimentations, fruitful partnerships, but also to difficulties in terms of how such legacy is managed and capitalised upon. Digital projects might require skills and resources that—as the project ends—might not be available anymore. Also, a lot depends on whether HCI work in museums is seen from the beginning as a one-off interesting experiment, or something that fits into a broader strategy of digital engagement that a museum might have, or even the beginning of new practices and approaches. In all these cases, what happens at the end of a project should be discussed and even planned for.

Regarding the future of HCI work in museums, it is difficult to predict what new technological trends might be emerging in the next number of years. Rather, it is important to think of which innovations could characterise *interaction* in museums. Already we have seen a shift from mainly visual and screen-based installations toward tangible, immersive, and full-body interactions, made possible by a variety of technologies and platforms (from motion sensing, to mobile AR, to the Internet of Things). We have also seen more complex types of visitor activities being supported via technology, including dedicated activities for groups of visitors or for families, which might hand different roles to different group members, various forms of "treasure hunt" and collection activities, storytelling approaches, creative activities that might engage visitors themselves in storytelling and content creation, and others. All of these do not necessarily depend on a particular technology, and can be implemented in various ways, but might become easier to realize with new upcoming technologies. Still, from the visitor perspective, and from the museum's viewpoint (usually wanting to create a memorable experience that conveys something meaningful), it is more the activity and experience that is important, ratherthan the technology itself.

References

Ackermann, E. (1996). Perspective-taking and object construction: Two keys to learning. In Y. Kafai and M. Resnick (eds.), *Constructionism in Practice*. Mahwah, NJ: Lawrence Erlbaum, (pp. 25–35). 42

Alexander, J., Wienke, L., and Tiongson, P. (2017). Removing the barriers of gallery one: A new approach to integrating art, interpretation, and technology, *Proceedings Museums and the Web*. New York: ACM. https://mw17.mwconf.org/paper/removing-the-barriers-of-gallery-one-a-new-approach-to-integrating-art-interpretation-and-technology/. 41

Ali, S., Koleva, B., Bedwell, B., and Benford, S. (2018). Deepening visitor engagement with museum exhibits through hand-crafted visual markers, *Proceedings DIS 2018*, New York: ACM, 523–534. DOI: 10.1145/3196709.3196786. 24

Allen, S. (2004). Designs for learning: Studying science museum exhibits that do more than entertain. *Science Education*, 88(1):17–33. DOI: 10.1002/sce.20016. 10

Allen-Greil, E., Edwards, S., Ludden, J., and Johnson, E. (2011). Social media and organizational change, *Proceedings Museums and The Web 2011*. https://www.museumsandtheweb.com/mw2011/papers/social_media_and_organizational_change. 78

Anderson, D., Storksdieck, M., and Spock, M. (2007). Understanding the long-term impacts of museum experiences. In Falk, J., Dierking, L., and Foutz, S. (eds.), *In Principle, in Practice – New Perspectives on Museums as Learning Institutions*. AltaMira Press. 58

Aoki, P. M., Grinter, R. E., Hurst, A., Szymanski, M. H., Thornton, J. D., and Woodruff, A. (2002). Sotto Voce: exploring the interplay of conversation and mobile audio spaces. *Proceedings of CHI 2002*. New York: ACM, pp. 431–438. DOI: 10.1145/503376.503454. 26

Ardito, C., Costabile, M. F., Lanzilotti, R., and Simeone, A. L. (2010). Combining multimedia resources for an engaging experience of cultural heritage. *Proceedings of the 2010 ACM Workshop on Social, Adaptive and Personalised Multimedia Interaction and Access* (SAPMIA '10), pp. 45–48. DOI: 10.1145/1878061.1878077. 97

Ardito, C., Costabile, M. F., De Angeli, A., Lanzilotti, R. (2012). Enriching archaeological parks with contextual sounds and mobile technology. *ACM Transactions on Computer-Human Interaction*, 19(4), Article 29:1–30. 97

Ardissono, L., Kuflik, T., and Petrelli, D. (2011). Personalization in cultural heritage: the road travelled and the one ahead. *User-Modelling and User-Adapted Interaction*, 22:(1–2):73–99. 26

Arnold-de Simine, S. (2013). *Mediating Memory in the Museum: Trauma, Empathy, Nostalgia*, Palgrave Macmillan. DOI: 10.1057/9781137352644. 12

Atkinson, R. (2013). *Museum Practice: How Are Museums Using Mobile*. Museums Association. https://www.museumsassociation.org/museumpractice/mobile-in-museums-2013/15102013-mobilesurvey-2013-results. 24

Avram, G., Ciolfi, L., Maye, L. (2019). Creating tangible interactions with cultural heritage: Lessons learned from a large scale, long-term co-design project. *CoDesign Journal*, Accepted. DOI: 10.1080/15710882.2019.1596288. 92

Bacci, F. and Pavani, F. (2014). "First hand," not "first eye" knowledge. Bodily experience in museums. In Levant, N. (ed.) *The Multisensory Museum: Cross-Disciplinary Perspectives on Touch, Sound*. Alvaro Pascual-Leone. 41, 56

Bailey-Ross, C. S., Gray, S., Hudson-Smith, A., Warwick, C., and Terras, M. (2012). Enhancing museum narratives with the QRator project: a Tasmanian devil, a Platypus and a dead man in a box. *Museums and the Web 2012*, San Diego. https://www.museumsandtheweb.com/mw2012/papers/enhancing_museum_narratives_with_the_qrator_pr. 74

Bamberger, Y. and Tali, T. (2008). An experience for the lifelong journey: The long-term effect of a class visit to a science centre. *Visitor Studies*, 11:2:198–212. DOI: 10.1080/10645570802355760. 112

Banerjee, A., Robert, R., and Horn, M. S. (2018). FieldGuide: Smartwatches in a multi-display museum environment. *Proceeding CHI EA '18 Extended Abstracts of the 2018 CHI Conference on Human Factors in Computing Systems*. Paper No. LBW061. New York: ACM. DOI: 10.1145/3170427.3188694. 34

Bannon, L., Benford, S., Bowers, J., and Heath, C. (2005). Hybrid design creates innovative museum experiences. *Communications of the ACM*, 48(3):62–65. DOI: 10.1145/1047671.1047706. 29

Barron, P. and Leask, A. (2017). Visitor engagement at museums: Generation Y and 'Lates' events at the National Museum of Scotland. *Museum Management and Curatorship*, 32(5):473–490. DOI: 10.1080/09647775.2017.1367259. 61

Bedford, L. (2014). *The Art of Museum Exhibitions: How Story and Imagination Create Aesthetic Experiences*. Walnut Creek, CA: Left Coast Press. 1, 7, 54

Beheshti, E., Kim, D., Ecanow, G., and Horn, M. S. (2017). Looking inside the wires: Understanding museum visitor learning with an augmented circuit exhibit. *Proceedings of the*

2017 CHI Conference on Human Factors in Computing Systems, New York: ACM, pp. 1583–1594. DOI: 10.1145/3025453.3025479. 48

Bekele, M. K., Pierdicca, R., Frontoni, E., Malinverni, E. S., and Gain, J. (2018). A survey of augmented, virtual, and mixed reality for cultural heritage. *Journal on Computing Cultural Heritage*, 11(2), Article 7. DOI: https://doi.org/10.1145/3145534. 43, 46

Bell, G. (2002). *Making Sense of Museums. The Museum as 'Cultural Ecology'*. Intel Labs. 2

Benford, S. and Giannachi, G. (2011). *Performing Mixed Reality*. The MIT Press. 28, 54

Benford, S., Crabtree, A., Flintham, M., Koleva, B., Tandavanitj, N., Farr, J. R., Giannachi, G., and Lindt, I. (2011). Creating the spectacle: Designing interactional trajectories through spectator interfaces, *ACM Transactions on Computer-Human Interaction* (TOCHI) 18(3), Article 11. DOI: 10.1145/1993060.1993061. 54

Benyon, D. (2013). *Designing Interactive Systems*, 3rd ed. Harlow: Pearson. 85

Best, K. (2012). Making museum tours better: understanding what a guided tour really is and what a tour guide really does. *Museum Management and Curatorship*, 27(1):35–52, DOI: 10.1080/09647775.2012.644695. 119

Birchfield, D., Mechtley, B., Hatton, S., and Thornburg, H. (2008). Mixed-reality learning in the art museum context. *Proceeding MM '08 Proceedings of ACM Conference on Multimedia*, New York: ACM, pp. 965–968. DOI: 10.1145/1459359.1459534. 53

Bitgood, S. (2013). *Attention and Value. Keys to Understanding Museum Visitors*. Walnut Creek, CA: Left Coast Press. 10

Bitgood, S. (2006). An analysis of visitor circulation: Movement patterns and the general value principle. *Curator*, 49:463–475. DOI: 10.1111/j.2151-6952.2006.tb00237.x. 104

Bitgood, S. (2011). *Social Design in Museums. The Psychology of Visitor Studies. Collected Essays Volume One*. MuseumsEtc. 104

Black, G. (2005). *The Engaging Museum*. London: Routledge. 75

Black, G. (2010). Embedding civil engagement in museums. *Museum Management and Curatorship*, 25(2):129–146. DOI: 10.1080/09647771003737257. 75

Block, F., Hammerman, J., Horn, M., Spiegel, A,. Christiansen, J., Phillips, B., Diamond, J., Evans, E. M., and Shen, C. (2015). Fluid grouping: Quantifying group engagement around interactive tabletop exhibits in the wild. *Proceedings of ACM CHI*. New York: ACM. DOI:10.1145/2702123.2702231. 9, 10

Bowers, J., Bannon, L., Fraser, M., Hindmarsh, J., Benford, S., Heath. C., Taxén, G., and Ciolfi, L. (2007). From the disappearing computer to living exhibitions: Shaping interactivity in museum settings. In Streitz, N., Kameas, A., and Mavrommati, I. (eds.), *The Disappearing Computer: Interaction Design, System Infrastructures and Applications for Smart Environments*. Heidelberg: Springer LNCS 4500. 29

Bratteteig, T. and Wagner, I. (2010). Spaces for participatory creativity. *Proceedings PDC 2010,*. New York: ACM, 51–60. DOI: 10.1145/1900441.1900449. 90

Bratteteig, T. and Wagner, I. (2014). *Disentangling Participation. Power and Decision-making in Participatory Design*. London: Springer. 91

Braun, V. and Clarke, V. (2006). Using thematic analysis in psychology. *Qualitative Research in Psychology*, 3(2):77–101. DOI: 10.1191/1478088706qp063oa. 113

Broadbent, J. and Marti, P. (1997). Location aware interactive guides: usability issues. In *Proceedings of the 1997 International Cultural Heritage Informatics Meeting. Archives and Museums Informatics*. https://www.museumsandtheweb.com/biblio/location_aware_mobile_interactive_guides_usability__0.html. 91

Bruckner, A. (2011). *Scenography/Szenografie: Making Spaces Talk, Projects 2002-2010*. Avedition Gmbh. 5, 54

Bryan, M. (2016). Google's new museum tours bring dinosaurs to life. *Endgadget*. https://www.engadget.com/2016/09/13/google-natural-history-art-culture-app/?guccounter=1. 44

Buxton, B., (2007). *Sketching User Experiences: Getting the Design Right and the Right Design*. Morgan Kaufman. 85

Byatt, A. (2005). Handbags and Baggage: the Visitors' board, audience assumptions and Women in Thatcher's Britain. *Proceedings of Re-Thinking Technology in Museums 2005*, University of Limerick, pp. 26–32. 67

Caulton, T. (1998). *Hands-On Exhibitions*. London: Routledge. DOI: 10.4324/9780203271513. 68

Champion, E. (2011). *Playing with the Past*. Human-Computer Interaction Series. London: Springer. 45

Champion, E. (2015). *Critical Gaming: Interactive History and Virtual Heritage*. Farnham, UK: Ashgate. 44

Chen, T.-K., Fang, H.-P., Tian, Y., Fang, H.-L., Li, Y.-J., Tseng, S.-H., and Miao, S.-E. (2011). Design and evaluation of social interfaces for cultural exhibitions of Chinese shadow puppetry. *IEEE 35th Annual Computer Software and Applications Conference*, pp. 346–347. DOI: 10.1109/COMPSAC.2011.52. 41

Chu, J. H., Clifton, P., Harley, D., Pavao, J., and Mazalek, A. (2015). Mapping place: Supporting cultural learning through a Lusaka-inspired tangible tabletop museum exhibit. *Proceed-*

ings of ACM TEI 2015, New York: ACM, pp. 261–268. DOI: 10.1145/2677199.2680559. 22

Chu, J. H., Harley, D., Kwan, J., McBride, M., and Mazalek, A. (2016). Sensing History: Contextualizing Artifacts with Sensory Interactions and Narrative Design. In *Proceedings of the 2016 ACM Conference on Designing Interactive Systems (DIS '16)*. New York, NY: ACM, pp. 1294–1302. DOI: 10.1145/2901790.2901829. 37, 56

Ciolfi, L., Avram, G., Maye, L., Dulake, N., Marshall, M.T., van Dijk, D., and McDermott, F. (2016). Articulating co-design in museums: Reflection on two participatory processes, *Proceedings of CSCW 2016*. New York: ACM, pp. 13–25. DOI: 10.1145/2818048.2819967. 93

Ciolfi, L., Bannon, L., and Fernström, M. (2001). Envisioning and evaluating 'Out-of-Storage' solution. In Bearman, D. and Garzotto, F. (eds.), *Proceedings of ICHIM01 International Cultural Heritage Informatics Meeting*. Milan. 20

Ciolfi, L., Bannon, L., and Fernström, M. (2008). Including visitor contributions in cultural heritage installations: Designing for participation. *Museum Management and Curatorship*, 23(4):4:353–365. DOI: 10.1080/09647770802517399. 71, 72, 75, 81

Ciolfi, L., Damala, A., Hornecker, E., Lechner, M., and Maye, L. (eds.) (2018). *Cultural Heritage Communities: Technologies and Challenges*. Informa UK/Routledge (Taylor and Francis). 2, 78

Ciolfi, L. and McLoughlin, M. (2011). Physical keys to digital memories: Reflecting on the role of tangible artefacts in "Reminisce". In Bearman, D. and Trant, J. (eds.), *Proceedings of Museums and the Web 2011*, *Museums and Archives Informatics*, pp. 197–208. 31, 115

Ciolfi, L. and McLoughlin, M. (2012). Designing for meaningful visitor engagement at a living history museum. *Proceedings of NordiCHI 2012*, New York: ACM. DOI: 10.1145/2399016.2399028. 81, 115

Ciolfi, L. and McLoughlin, M. (2017). Supporting place-specific interaction through a physical/digital Assembly. *Human-Computer Interaction*, 33(5-6):499–543. 31, 72, 106, 114, 118

Ciolfi, L., Petrelli, D., McDermott, F., Avram, G., and van Dijk, D. (2015). Co-design to empower cultural heritage professionals as technology designers: The meSch project. In Bihanic, D. (ed.), *Empowering Users Through Design*. London: Springer, pp. 213–224. DOI: 10.1007/978-3-319-13018-7_12.

Claisse, C., Ciolfi, L., and Petrelli, D. (2017). Containers of Stories: Using co-design and digital augmentation to empower the museum community and create novel experiences of heritage at a house museum. *The Design Journal*, 20(sup1): *Design for Next: Pro-*

ceedings of the 12th European Academy of Design Conference, pp. S2906–S2918. DOI: 10.1080/14606925.2017.1352801. 93, 94

Claisse, C., Petrelli, D., Marshall, M., and Ciolfi, L. (2018). Multisensory interactive storytelling to augment the visit of a historical house museum. *Proceedings of Digital HERITAGE 2018*, San Francisco. pp. 26–30. 55, 56, 57, 106

Clarke, L. (2013). *An Interview with the Riverside Transport Museum in Glasgow on their Design Approach to Interactive Installations.* http://www.mesch-project.eu/an-interview-with-the-riverside-transport-museum-in-glasgow-on-their-design-approach-to-interactive-installations/. 84, 89

Clarke, L. and Hornecker, E. (2012). Designing and studying a multimodal painting installation in a cultural centre for children. *Physicality 2012, 4th International Workshop on Physicality, 11*, University of Birmingham, UK. 86

Clarke, L. and Hornecker, E. (2013). Experience, engagement and social interaction at a steam locomotive multimodal interactive museum exhibit. Proceeedings of the *ACM CHI'13 Extended Abstracts*, New York: ACM, pp. 613–618. DOI: 10.1145/2468356.2468464. 116

Clarke, L. and Hornecker, E. (2015). Social activities with offline tangibles at an interactive painting exhibit in a children's cultural centre. *Proceedings of British HCI'15*, Lincoln, UK. New York: ACM. pp. 82–90. DOI: 10.1145/2783446.2783568. 86

Clarke, R., Vines, J., Wright, P., Bartindale, T., Shearer, J., McCarthy, J., and Olivier, P. (2015). MyRun: balancing design for reflection, recounting and openness in a museum-based participatory platform. *British HCI Conference 2015*. New York: ACM. https://dl.acm.org/citation.cfm?id=2783569&CFID=994001545&CFTOKEN=66424774. 65, 68

Cooper, G. and Bowers, J. (1995). Representing the user: notes on the disciplinary rhetoric of human-computer interaction. In Thomas, P. J. (ed.) *The Social and Interactional Dimensions of Human-Computer Interfaces*. Cambridge: Cambridge University Press, pp. 48–66. 85

Cosley, D., Baxter, J., Lee, S., Alson, B., Nomura, S., Adams, P., Sarabu, C., and Gay, G. (2009). A tag in the hand: supporting semantic, social, and spatial navigation in museums. *Proceedings of CHI '09*, New York: ACM, pp. 1953–1962. DOI: 10.1145/1518701.1518999. 27

Dale, B. (2016). The Cooper-Hewitt's connected pen brings visitors back - Online, *Observer*, 02/09/2016. https://observer.com/2016/02/20-percent-of-this-smithsonian-museums-connected-pen-users-come-back-to-its-site/. 33

Dancstep, T., Gutwill, J. P., and Sindorf, L. (2015). Comparing the visitor experience at immersive and tabletop exhibits. *Curator* 58(4):401–422. DOI: 10.1111/cura.12137. 42, 88

Damala, A., Cubaud, P., Bationo, A., Houlier, P., and Marchal, I. (2008). Bridging the gap between the digital and the physical: Design and evaluation of a mobile augmented reality guide for the museum visit. *Proceedings of the 3rd international conference on Digital Interactive Media in Entertainment and Arts*, pp. 120–127. DOI: 10.1145/1413634.1413660. 46

Damala, A., van der Vaart, M., Clarke, L., Hornecker, E., Avram, G., Kockelkorn, H., and Ruthven, I. (2016). Evaluating tangible and multisensory museum visiting experiences: lessons learned from the meSch project. Proceedings of *Museums and the Web 2016*. https://mw2016.museumsandtheweb.com/paper/evaluating-tangible-and-multisensory-museum-visiting-experiences-lessons-learned-from-the-mesch-project/. 105, 106, 117

Davies, M. and Heath, C. (2014). "Good" organisational reasons for "ineffectual" research: Evaluating summative evaluation of museums and galleries. *Cultural Trends*, 23(1). DOI: 10.1080/09548963.2014.862002. 7, 9, 14, 104, 110, 113, 115, 122

Davis, N. (2015). Don't just look – smell, feel, and hear art. Tate's new way of experiencing paintings. *The Observer*, 22. https://www.theguardian.com/artanddesign/2015/aug/22/tate-sensorium-art-soundscapes-chocolates-invisible-rain. 57

Diamond, S. (2005). Participation, flow and the redistribution of authorship: The challenges of collaborative exchange and new media curatorial practice. *Proceedings of Museums and the Web 2005*: Selected papers from an international conference, Bearman, D. and Trant, J. (eds.) Philadelphia: Archives and Museums Informatics. 68, 73

Diamond, J., Horn, M., and Uttal, D. H. (2016). *Practical Evaluation Guide. Tools for Museums and Other Informal Educational Settings*. 3d ed. Rowman and Littlefield. 122

Dim, E. and Kuflik, S. (2014). Automatic detection of social behaviour of museum visitor pairs. *ACM Transactions on Interactive Intelligent Systems*, 4(4): Article 17. DOI: 10.1145/2662869. 107

Dima, M., Hurcombe, L., and Wright, M. (2014). Touching the past: Haptic augmented reality for museum artefacts. In Shumaker R., Lackey S. (eds), *Virtual. Augmented, and Mixed Reality. Applications of Virtual and Augmented Reality*. VAMR 2014. Lecture Notes in Computer Science, 8526:3–14. Springer, Cham. DOI: 10.1007/978-3-319-07464-1_1. 49

Dindler, C., Iversen, O. S., Smith, R., and Veerasawmy, R. (2010). Participatory design at the museum: inquiring into children's everyday engagement in cultural heritage. *Proceedings of the 22nd Conference of the Computer-Human Interaction Special Interest Group of Australia on Computer-Human Interaction* (OZCHI '10), New York: ACM, pp. 72–79. DOI: 10.1145/1952222.1952239. 91

Durrant, A., Rowland, D., Kirk, D. S., Benford, S., Fischer, J., and McAuley, D. (2011). Automics: souvenir generating photoware for theme parks. *Proceedings CHI '11*, New York: ACM *(2011)*, pp. 1767–1776. DOI: 10.1145/1978942.1979199. 59

Economou, M. (2010). The evaluation of museum multimedia applications. In Parry, R. (ed.) *Museums in a Digital Age*. Readers in Museum Studies, pp. 391–405. 6

Economou, M. and Meintani, E. (2011). Promising beginning? Evaluating museum mobile phone apps. *Proceedings of Rethinking Technology in Museums 2011: Emerging Experiences*, Limerick, Ireland, pp. 26–27, May. 26

Elinich, K. (2014). Augmented reality for interpretive and experiential learning. *Proceedings of Museums and the Web 2014*. http://mw2014.museumsandtheweb.com/paper/augmented-reality-for-interpretive-and-experiential-learning/. 46

Ellenbogen, K., Luke, J., and Dierking, L. (2004). Family learning research in museums: An emerging disciplinary matrix? *Science Education* 88(1):48–58. DOI: 10.1002/sce.20015. 10

Everett, E. and Barrett, M. S. (2009). Investigating sustained visitor/museum relationships: Employing narrative research in the field of museum visitor studies. *Visitor Studies*, 12(1):2–15. DOI: 10.1080/10645570902769084. 61

Falk, J. H. (2009). *Identity and the Museum Visitor Experience*. Routledge. 7

Falk, J. H. and Dierking, L. D. (1992). *The Museum Experience*. Howells House. 1, 119

Falk, J. H. and Dierking, L. D. (2013). *The Museum Experience Revisited*. Walnut Creek, CA: Left Coast Press. 1, 6, 54, 119

Falk, J. H. and Dierking, L. D. (2000). *Learning from Museums: Visitor Experiences and the Making of Meaning*. AltaMira Press. 10, 104

Falk, J. H., Dierking, L. D., and Adams, M. (2006). Living in a learning society: Museums and freechoice learning. In Macdonald, S. (ed.) *A Companion to Museum Studies*. Blackwell Publishing. Blackwell Reference Online. July 5. DOI: 10.1002/9780470996836.ch19. 9, 10, 12, 104

Falk, J. H., Moussouri, T., and Coulson, D. (1998). The effect of visitors 'agendas on museum learning. *Curator: The Museum Journal*, 41(2):107–120. DOI: 10.1111/j.2151-6952.1998.tb00822.x. 121

Ferris, K., Bannon, L., Ciolfi, L., Gallagher, P., Hall, T., and Lennon, M. (2004). Shaping experiences in the Hunt Museum: A design case study. *Proceedings of DIS04*. New York: ACM. DOI: 10.1145/1013115.1013144. 31, 72

Filippini-Fantoni, S. and Bowe, J. P. (2008). Mobile multimedia: Reflections from ten years of practice. In Tallon, L. and K. Walker (eds.), *Digital Technologies and the Museum Experience*. AltaMira Press. 26

Flintham, M., Benford, S., Anastasi, R., Hemmings, T., Crabtree, A., Greenhalgh, C., Tandavanjti, C., Adams, M., and Farr, J. R. (2003). Where on-line meets on the streets: experiences with mobile mixed reality games. *Proceeding CHI '03 Proceedings of the SIGCHI Conference on Human Factors in Computing Systems*, New York: ACM, pp. 569–576. DOI: 10.1145/642611.642710.

Flintham, M., Greenhalgh, C., Lodge, T., Chamberlain, A., Paxton, M., Jacobs, R., Watkins, M., and Shackford, R. (2011). A case study of exploding places, a mobile location-based game. *Proceedings of the 8th International Conference on Advances in Computer Entertainment Technology*, Article 30. New York: ACM. DOI: 10.1145/2071423.2071460. 54

Fosh, L., Benford, S., Reeves, S., Koleva, B., and Brundell, P. (2013). See me, feel me, touch, me, hear me: trajectories and interpretation in a sculpture garden. *Proceedings of CHI 2013*, New York: ACM, pp. 149–158. DOI: 10.1145/2470654.2470675. 28, 29

Fosh, L., Benford, S., Reeves, S., and Koleva, B. (2014). Gifting personal interpretations in galleries. *Proceedings of CHI 2014*, New York: ACM, pp. 625-634. DOI: 10.1145/2556288.2557259. 74

Fraser, M., Stanton, D., Ng, K. H., Beneford, S., O'Malley, C., Bowers, J., Taxén, G., Ferris, K., and Hindmarsh, J. (2003). Assembling history: Achieving coherent experiences with diverse technologies. *Proceedings of ECSCW 2003*, Norwell MA: Kluwer, pp. 179–198. DOI: 10.1007/978-94-010-0068-0_10. 29, 30, 31

Fraser, M., Stanton, D., Ng, K. H.., Beneford, S., O'Malley, C., Bowers, J., Taxén, G., Ferris, K., and Hindmarsh, J. (2004). Paper as glue: Using tagged paper to assemble diverse Displays into coherent visiting experiences. https://www.researchgate.net/publication/242091766_Paper_as_Glue_Using_Tagged_Paper_to_Assemble_Diverse_Displays_into_Coherent_Visiting_Experiences. 31

Fuks, H., Moura, H., Cardador, D., Vega, K., Ugulino, W., and Barbato, M. (2012). Collaborative museums: an approach to co-design. *Proceedings of the ACM 2012 conference on Computer. Supported Cooperative Work* (CSCW '12), New York: ACM, pp. 681–684. DOI: 10.1145/2145204.2145307. 91

Galani, A. and Chalmers, M. (2003). Far away is close at hand: shared mixed reality museum experiences for local and remote museum companions. In *Proceedings of the Seventh International Cultural Heritage Informatics Meeting* (ICHIM 2003), Paris. 53

Galani, A., Maxwell, D., Mazel, A., and Sharpe, K. (2013). Situating cultural technologies outdoors: Empathy in the design of mobile interpretation of rock art in rural Britain. In Ch'ng, E., Gaffney, V., Chapman, H. (eds.), *Visual Heritage in the Digital Age*. London: Springer, pp. 183–204. DOI: 10.1007/978-1-4471-5535-5_10. 27, 29

Gammon. B. and Burch, A. (2008). Designing digital mobile experiences. In Tallon, L. and Walker, K. (eds.) *Digital Technologies and the Museum Experience*. Altamira Press, pp. 35–60. 6, 75

Geroimenko, V. (ed.). (2018). *Augmented Reality Art. From an Emerging Technology to a Novel Creative Medium*. London: Springer. DOI: 10.1007/978-3-319-69932-5. 48

Ghiani, G., Paternò, F., and Spano, L. D. (2009). Cicero designer: An environment for end-user development of multi-device museum guides. *2nd International Symposium on End-User Development (IS-EUD '09)*, pp. 265–274. *Lecture Notes in Computer Science*, vol. 5435. Springer, Berlin, Heidelberg. 97

Giaccardi, E. (2012). *Heritage and Social Media*. London: Routledge. DOI: 10.4324/9780203112984. 65

Giaccardi, E. and Fischer, G. (2008). Creativity and evolution: a metadesign perspective. *Digital Creativity*. 19(1):19–32. DOI: 10.1080/14626260701847456. 94

Giaccardi, E. and Palen, L. (2008). The social production of heritage through cross-media interaction: Making place for place-making, *International Journal of Heritage Studies*, 14(3):281–197. DOI: 10.1080/13527250801953827. 73, 74

Gillam, S. (2017). Spotlight VR/AR: Innovation in transformative storytelling. *Proceedings of Museums and the Web 2017*. https://mw17.mwconf.org/paper/spotlight-vrar-innovation-in-transformative-storytelling/. 43, 45, 48

Gokcigdem, E. M. (2016). *Fostering Empathy Through Museums*. Latham, MD: Rowman and Littlefield. 12

Goodman, E., Kuniavsky, M., and Moed, A. (2012). *Observing the User Experience: A Practitioner's Guide to User Research*. San Francisco: Morgan Kaufman. 85

Grabill, J. T., Pigg, S., and Wittenauer, K. (2009). Take two: A study of the co-creation of knowledge on museum 2.0 sites, *Proceedings Museums and the Web 2009*. https://www.museumsandtheweb.com/mw2009/papers/grabill/grabill.html. 78

Greenbaum, J. and Kyng, M. (1991). *Design at Work: Cooperative Design of Computer Systems*, Hillsdale NJ: CRC Press. 90

Grinter, R. E., Aoki, P. M., Hurst, A., Symanski, M. H., Thornton, J. D., and Woodruff, A. (2002). Revisiting the visit: Understanding how technology can shape the museum visit. *Proceed-*

ings of ACM CSCW 2002, New York: ACM, pp. 146–155. DOI: 10.1145/587078.587100. 26

Gutwill, J. P. and Allen, S. (2010). *Group Inquiry at Science Museum Exhibits. Getting Visitors to Ask Juicy Questions.* Walnut Creek, CA: Exploratorium/Left Coast Press. 10

Gutwin, C. and Greenberg, S. (2002). A descriptive framework of workspace awareness for real-time groupware. *Journal Computer Supported Cooperative Work* 11(3):411–446. DOI: 10.1023/A:1021271517844. 9

Halloran, J., Hornecker, E., Fitzpatrick, G., Weal, M., Millard, D., Michaelides, D., Cruikshank, D., and De Roure, D. (2006). Unfolding understandings: Co-designing UbiComp in situ, over time. *Proceedings of DIS 2006* (Designing Interactive Systems), New York: ACM Press (2006). pp. 109–118. 93

Halskov, K. and Dalsgaard, P. (2011). Using 3-D projection to bring a statue to life. *Interactions.* 18(3):60–65. DOI: 10.1145/1962438.1962452. 50

Harley, D., McBride, M., Ho Chu, J., Kwan, J., Nolan, J., and Mazalek, A. (2016). Sensing context: Reflexive design principles for intersensory museum interactions. *MW2016: Museums and the Web 2016.* Los Angeles. https://mw2016.museumsandtheweb.com/paper/sensing-context-reflexive-design-principles-for-inter-sensory-museum-interactions/. 56

Harrison, S., Minneman, S., and Balsamo, A. (2001). How of XFR "experiments in the Future of Reading." *Interactions.* 8(3):31–41. DOI: 10.1145/369825.369830. 18

Heath, C., and Luff, P. (2000). Technology in Action. Cambridge: Cambridge University Press. DOI: 10.1017/CBO9780511489839. 118

Heath, C., Luff, P., vom Lehn, D., Hindmarsh, J., and Cleverly, J. (2002). Crafting participation: Designing ecologies, configuring experience. *Visual Communication.* 1(1):9–33. DOI: 10.1177/147035720200100102. 70, 106, 118

Heath, C., Hindmarsh, J., and Luff, P. (2010). *Video in Qualitative Research.* Sage Publications. 116, 118

Heath, C. and vom Lehn, D. (2002). Misconstruing interactivity. In *Proceedings of Interactive Learning in Museums of Art.* London: V&A Museum. 9

Heath, C. and vom Lehn, D. (2004). Configuring reception: (Dis-)regarding the 'Spectator' in museums and galleries. *Theory, Culture and Society,* 21(6):43–65. DOI: 10.1177/0263276404047415. 118

Heath, C., vom Lehn, D., and Osborne, J. (2005). Interaction and interactives: collaboration and participation with computer-based exhibits. *Public Understanding of Science*, 14(1):91–101. DOI: 10.1177/0963662505047343. 8, 10. 26

Hein, G. E. (1998). *Learning in the Museum*, London, New York: Routledge. 11

Heumann Gurian, E. (2006). *Civilizing the Museum*. London: Routledge. 68, 123

Hillman, T., Weilenmann, A., and Jungselius, B. (2012). Creating live experiences with real and stuffed animals: The use of mobile technologies in museums. *Proceedings of The Transformative Museum, DREAM* (Danish Research Centre on Education and Advanced Media Materials). 27, 75

Hindmarsh, J., Heath, C., vom Lehn, D., and Cleverly, J. (2002). Creating assemblies: Aboard the Ghost Ship. *Proceedings of the 2002 ACM Conference on Computer Supported Cooperative Work,* New York: ACM Press, pp. 156–165. DOI: 10.1145/587078.587101. 70, 81

Hindmarsh, J., Heath, C., vom Lehn, D., and Celeverly, J. (2005), Creating assemblies in public environments: Social interaction, interactive exhibits and CSCW, *Computer Supported Cooperative Work*, 14(1):1–41. 106

Hinrichs, U. and Carpendale, S. (2011). Gestures in the wild: studying multi-touch gesture sequences on interactive tabletop exhibits. *Proceedings of CHI 2011*, New York: ACM, pp. 3023–3032. DOI: 10.1145/1978942.1979391. 21, 22

Hooper-Greenhill, E. (2006). Studying visitors. In Macdonald, S. (ed.) *A Companion to Museum Studies* : Blackwell, Chapter 2. DOI: 10.1002/9780470996836.ch22. 103

Horn, M. S., Solovey, E. T., Crouser, R. J., and Jacob, R. J. K. (2009).Comparing the use of tangible and graphical programming interfaces for informal science education. *Proceedings of CHI'09*. New York: ACM, pp. 975–984. DOI: 10.1145/1518701.1518851. 35, 118

Horn, M. S., Leong, Z. A., Block, F., Diamond, J., Evans, E. M., Phillips, B., and Shen, C. (2012). Of BATs and APEs: An interactive tabletop game for natural history museums. *Proceedings of CHI Extended Abstracts 2014*. New York: ACM. DOI: 10.1145/2207676.2208355. 3, 11

Horn, M. S., Weintrop, D., and Routman, E. (2014). Programming in the pond: a tabletop computer programming exhibit. *CHI EA 14*, New York: ACM,. pp. 1417–1422. DOI: 10.1145/2559206.2581237. 22

Hornecker, E. (2008). "I don't understand it either, but it is cool" - Visitor interactions with a multi-touch table in a museum. *Proceedings of IEEE Tabletop 2008*, pp. 121–128. 20, 21, 106

Hornecker, E. (2010). Interactions around a contextually embedded system. *Proceedings of TEI'10*. New York: ACM, pp. 169–176. DOI: 10.1145/1709886.1709916. 9, 39, 106, 115, 118

Hornecker, E. (2016). The to-and-fro of sense making: Supporting users' active indexing in museums. *ACM Transactions on Computer-Human Interaction* (TOCHI) 23(2), Article 10. 39, 40, 119

Hornecker, E. and Buur, J. (2006). Getting to grips with tangible interaction, *Proceedings of the CHI 2006 SIGCHI Conference on Human Factors in Computing Systems*. New York: ACM, pp. 437–446. DOI: 10.1145/1124772.1124838. 34

Hornecker, E., and Nicol, E. (2011). Toward the wild: Evaluating museum installations in semi-realistic situations. *Proceedings of Re-thinking Technology in Museums 2011 Conference*. University of Limerick, Ireland, pp. 49–60. 6, 87, 88, 89

Hornecker, E. and Nicol, E. (2012). What do lab-based user studies tell us about in-the-wild behaviour? Insights from a study of museum interactives. *Proceedings of Designing Interactive Systems* (DIS'12), New York: ACM, pp. 358–367. 11, 88, 89, 118

Hornecker, E. and Stifter, M. (2004). *Evaluationsstudie Ausstellung medien.welten des Technischen Museums Wien—Interaktives Leitsystem medien.welten. Qualitative und Quantitative Auswertung*. TU Vienna (internal report). 109

Hornecker, E. and Stifter, M. (2006a). Learning from interactive museum installations about interaction design for public settings. *Proceedings of OzCHI 2006*. New York: ACM, pp. 135–142. DOI: 10.1145/1228175.1228201. 10, 20, 69, 105, 112

Hornecker, E. and Stifter, M. (2006b). Digital backpacking in the museum with a SmartCard. *Proceedings of CHINZ (7th Annual Conference of the NZ ACM Special Interest Group)*. New York: ACM, pp. 99–107. 33, 59, 105, 109

Hsieh, C., Hung, Y-P., Ben-Ezra, M., and Hsieh, H. F. (2013). Viewing Chinese art on an interactive tabletop. *IEEE Computer Graphics and Applications*, 33(3): 16–21. DOI: 10.1109/MCG.2013.50. 22

Hudson-Smith, A., Gray, S., Ross, D., Bartel, R., De Jode, M., Warwick, C., and Terras, M. (2012). Experiments with the Internet of Things in museum space: QRator. *UbiComp '12: Proceedings of the 2012 Conference on Ubiquitous Computing*. New York: ACM, pp. 1183–1184. DOI: 10.1145/2370216.2370469. 74

Humphrey, T., Gutwill, J., and Exploratorium APE Team. (2005). *Fostering Active Prolonged Engagement. The Art of Creating APE Exhibits*. Exploratorium/Left Coast Press. 115, 120

Hunsucker, A. J., Baumgartner, E., and McClingon, K. (2018). Evaluating an AR-based museum experience. *Interactions*, XXV(4): 66–68. DOI: 10.1145/3215844. 49

Ishii, H. and Ullmer, B. (1997). Tangible bits: Toward seamless interfaces between people, bits and atoms. *Proceedings of the ACM CHI 97 Human Factors in Computing Systems Conference*, New York: ACM, pp. 234–241. DOI: 10.1145/258549.258715. 34

Iversen, O. S., Smith, R. C., and Dindler, C. (2017). Child as protagonist: Expanding the role of children in participatory design, *Proceedings IDC 2017*, New York: ACM, pp. 27–37. DOI: 10.1145/3078072.3079725. 91, 94

Johnson, L. A., Becker, S., Cumins, M., Estrada, V., Freeman, A., and Ludgate, H. (2012). *The NMC Horizon Report: 2012 Museum Edition*. Austin TX: The New Media Consortium. 40

Jürgs, A. (2017). *Virtual Reality in Museums. When Dinosaurs Come to Life*, https://www.goethe.de/ins/us/en/kul/tec/20949031.html. 44, 45

Kavanagh, G. (2000). *Dream Spaces: Memory and the Museum*. London: Leicester University Press. 2

Kelly, L., Savage, G., Griffin, J., and Tonkin, S. (2004). *Knowledge Quest: Australian Families Visit Museums*, Sydney: Australian Museum. 9

Kelly, L. (2004). Evaluation, research and communities of practice: Program evaluation in museums. *Archival Science*, 4(1–2):45–69. DOI: 10.1007/s10502-005-6990-x. 8, 86, 122

Kennedy, M. (2018). V&A Launches Quant Appeal for Exhibition on 60s Fashion Pioneer. https://www.theguardian.com/artanddesign/2018/jun/07/va-launches-quant-appeal-for-exhibition-on-60s-fashion-pioneer. 77

Kidd, J. (2014). *Museums in the New Mediascape*. London: Ashgate. 17, 65, 68, 78

Kidd, J. (2018a). Immersive' heritage encounters. *The Museum Review*, 3(1). http://articles.themuseumreview.org/tmr_vol3no1_kidd. 27, 28, 54

Kidd, J. (2018b). Digital media ethics and museum communication. In Drotner, K., Dziekan, V., Parry, R, and Schrøder, K. C. (eds.) *The Routledge handbook of Museums, Media and Communication*, London: Routledge, Section III.2, pp. 193–204. DOI: 10.4324/9781315560168-16. 78

Koleva, B., Egglestone, S. R., Schnädelbach, H., Glover, K., Greenhalgh, C., Rodden, T., and Dade-Robertson, M. (2009). Supporting the creation of hybrid museum experiences. *Proceedings of the SIGCHI Conference on Human Factors in Computing Systems* (CHI '09), New York: ACM, pp. 1973–1982. DOI: 10.1145/1518701.1519001. 96

Kollmann, E. K. (2007). The effect of broken exhibits on the experiences of visitors at a science museum. *Visitor Studies*, 10/2:178–191. DOI: 10.1080/10645570701585251. 13, 83, 112

Kourakis, S. and Parés, N. (2010). Us hunters: interactive communication for young cavemen. *Proceedings of the 9th International Conference on Interaction Design and Children* (IDC '10). New York: ACM, pp. 89–97. DOI: 10.1145/1810543.1810554. 19, 21

Kucsma, J., Reiss, K., and Sidman, A. (2010). Using Omeka to build digital collections: The METRO case study. *D-Lib Magazine* March/April 2010, 16(3/4). 97

Kuutti, K. (2001). "Hunting for the Lost User: From Sources of Errors to Active Actors – And Beyond." Paper written for the Cultural Usability – seminar, Media Lab, University of Art and Design Helsinki, May 4. http://www.mlab.uiah.fi/culturalusability/papers/Kuutti_paper.html.

Lackoi, K., Patsou, M., and Chatterjee, H.J. et al. (2016). *Museums for Health and Wellbeing*. A preliminary report, National Alliance for Museums, Health and Wellbeing. https://museumsandwellbeingalliance.wordpress.com. 57

Lane, C. and Parry, N. (2003). The memory machine: Sound and memory at the British Museum. *Proceedings of ICHIM03*. Philadelphia: Archives and Museums Informatics. 69

Lanir, J., Kuflik, T., Dim, E., Wecker, A. J., and Stock, O. (2013). The influence of a location-aware mobile guide on museum visitors' behaviour. *Interacting with Computers*, 25(6):443–460. DOI: 10.1093/iwc/iwt002. 26

vom Lehn, D., Heath, C., and Hindmarsh, J. (2002). Video-based field studies in museums and galleries. *Visitor Studies Today* 5:15–23. 116

vom Lehn, D., Heath, C. (2003). Displacing the object: Mobile technologies and interpretive resources. *Proceedings of ICHIM03, International Cultural Heritage Informatics Meeting*, France. 26

vom Lehn, D., Hindmarsh, J., Luff, P., and Heath, C. (2007). Engaging constable: Revealing art with new technology. *Proceedings of CHI 2007*. New York: ACM, pp. 148–149. DOI: 10.1145/1240624.1240848. 9, 118

Levent, N. and McRainey, D. L. (2014). Touch and narrative in art and history museums. In Levent, N. and Pascual, A. (eds.) *The Multisensory Museum*. Lanham, MD: Rowman & Littlefield. 55, 56

Levent, N. and Pascual, A. (eds.) (2014). *The Multisensory Museum. Cross-Disciplinary Perspectives on Touch, Sound, Smell, Memory, and Space*. Rowman and Littlefield. 1, 54

Lieberman, H., Paternò, F., Klann, M., and Wulf, V. (2006). End-user development: An emerging paradigm. In Lieberman, H., Paternò, F., Klann, M., and Wulf, V. (eds.) *End

User Development. Dordrecht, The Netherlands: Kluwer Academic Publishers. DOI: 10.1007/1-4020-5386-X_1. 94

Lister, J. (2018). "We Want Quant! Help Us Bring to Life the First Mary Quant Exhibition in 50 Years." https://www.vam.ac.uk/blog/news/we-want-quant-help-us-bring-to-life-the-first-mary-quant-exhibition-in-50-years. 77

Loparev, A., Westendorf, L., Flemings, M., Cho, J., Littrell, R., Scholze, A., and Shaer, O. (2016). BacPack for new frontiers: A tangible tabletop museum exhibit exploring synthetic biology, *Proceedings of ISS 2016, International Conference on Interactive Surfaces and Spaces*, New York: ACM, pp. 481–484. DOI: 10.1145/2992154.2996878. 22

Luke, J., Stein, J., Foutz, S., and Adams, M. (2007). Research to practice: Testing a tool for assessing critical thinking in art museum programs. *Journal of Museum Education*, 32:123–136. DOI: 10598650.2007.11510564. 106, 120

Lyons, L., Tissenbaum, M., Berland, M., Eydt, R., Wieglus, L., and Mechtley, A. (2015). Designing visible engineering: Supporting tinkering performances in museums. *Proceedings of the 14th Intl. Conference on Interaction Design and Children*, New York: ACM, pp. 49–58. DOI: 10.1145/2771839.2771845. 22

Ma, J., Sindorf, L., Liao, I., and Frazier. J. (2015). Using a tangible versus a multi-touch graphical user interface to support data exploration at a museum exhibit. *Proceedings of TEI 2015*. New York: ACM, pp. 33–39. DOI: 10.1145/2677199.2680555. 35

Macdonald, S. (2006). Expanding museum studies: An introduction. In Macdonald, S. (ed.). *A Companion to Museum Studies*. Blackwell Publishing. DOI: 10.1002/9780470996836. ch1. 2, 5

MacDonald, S. (2007). Interconnecting: museum visiting and exhibition design. *CoDesign*, 3(suppl 1):149–162. DOI: 10.1080/15710880701311502. 1, 7

Madsen, J. B. and Madsen, C. B. (2016). Handheld visual representation of a castle chapel ruin. *Journal on Computing and Cultural Heritage* (JOCCH) 9(1), Article 6. 49, 110

Malinverni, L. and Pares, N. (2014). Learning of abstract concepts through full-body interaction: A systematic review. *Educational Technology and Society*. 17:100–116. 42

Maquil V., Moll C., and Martins J. (2017). In the footsteps of Henri Tudor: Creating batteries on a tangible interactive workbench. *Proceedings of the 2017 ACM International Conference on Interactive Surfaces and Spaces* (ISS '17), New York: ACM, pp. 252–259. DOI: 10.1145/3132272.3134115. 36, 37, 87, 88

Marshall, M., Dulake, N., Ciolfi, L., Duranti, D., and Petrelli, D. (2016). Using tangible smart replicas as controls for an interactive museum exhibition. *Proceedings of TEI 2016 Conference on Tangible, Embedded and Embodied Interaction*, New York: ACM, pp. 159–167. DOI: 10.1145/2839462.2839493. 38, 109, 118

Martin, D. (2000). Audio guides. *Museum Practice*, 5(1):71–81. 23

Marttila, S. and Botero, A. (2017). Infrastructuring for cultural commons. *CSCW Journal*, 26:97–133. DOI: 10.1007/s10606-017-9273-1. 78

Mason, M. (2016). The MIT Museum glassware prototype: Visitor experience exploration for designing smart glasses. *Journal on Computing and Cultural Heritage* (JOCCH). 9(3), Article 12. DOI: 10.1145/2872278. 46

Massung, E. (2012). Visitor reception to location-based interpretation at archaeological and heritage sites. In Chrysanthy, A., Flores, M., and Papadopoulos, D. (eds.) *Thinking Beyond the Tool: Archaeological Computing and the Interpretive Process*; BAR International Series, Oxford, UK: Archaeopress. 29

Maye, L., McDermott, F., Ciolfi, L., and Avram, G. (2014). Interactive exhibitions design: what can we learn from cultural heritage professionals? *Proceedings of NordiCHI '14*. New York: ACM, pp. 598–607. DOI: 10.1145/2639189.2639259. 13, 14, 84

Maye, L., Bouchard, D., Avram, G., and Ciolfi, L. (2017). Supporting cultural Hheritage professionals adopting and shaping interactive technologies in museums. *Proceedings of DIS 2017*, New York: ACM, pp. 221–232. 93, 106

Mcdermott, F., Avram, G., Clarke, L., and Hornecker, E. (2013). The challenges and opportunities faced by cultural heritage professionals in designing interactive exhibits. Presented at *NODEM 2013 Conference*, Stockholm (Nordic Digital Excellence in Museums Conference). 14, 95

McGookin, D., Vazquez-Alvarez, Y., Brewster, S., and Bergstrom-Lehtovirta, J. (2012). Shaking the dead: Multimodal location based experiences for un-stewarded archaeological sites. *Proceedings of NordiCHI 2012*, New York: ACM, 199–208.. DOI: 10.1145/2399016.2399048. 27, 28

McGookin, D., Tahiroglu, K., Vaittinen, T., Kyto, M., Monastero, B., and Vasquez, J. C. (2017), Exploring seasonality in mobile cultural heritage. *Proceedings of ACM CHI 2017*, New York: ACM, pp. 6101–6105. DOI: 10.1145/3025453.3025803. 29

McLean, K. (1993). *Planning for People in Museum Exhibitions*. Washington D.C.: Association of Science and Technology Centres. 68

Meier, A. (2017). "Visitors Were Invited to Curate a Museum of Modern Nature and Here's What Sprouted," https://hyperallergic.com/391720/museum-of-modern-nature-wellcome-collection/. 77

Mine, M., Rose, D., Yang, B., van Baar, J., and Grundhöfer, A. (2012). Projection-based Augmented reality in Disney theme parks. *IEEE Computer* July 2012. pp. 32–40. 49

Monastero, B., McGookin, D., and Torre, G. (2016). Wandertroper: supporting aesthetic engagement with everyday surroundings through soundscape augmentation. *MUM '16 Proceedings of the 15th International Conference on Mobile and Ubiquitous Multimedia*, New York: ACM, pp. 129–140. 56

Mullen, E. and Tuohy, P. (2002). Exhibiting communications: Digital narratives at the National Library of Medicine. In Bearman, D. and Trant, J. (eds.) *Museums and the Web 2002: Selected Papers from an International Conference*, Pittsburgh: Archives and Museum Informatics. http://www.archimuse.com/mw2002/papers/mullen/mullen.html. 69

Muntean, R., Antle, A. N., Matkin, B., Hennessy, K., Rowley, S., and Wilson, J. (2017). Designing cultural values into interaction. *Proceedings of CHI 2017*, New York: ACM. DOI: 10.1145/3025453.3025908. 36

Mylonakis, J. and Kendristakis, E. (2006). Evaluation of museum service quality: A research study of museums and galleries visitors' satisfaction. *Tourism and Hospitality Management*, 12(2):37–54. https://hrcak.srce.hr/file/267067. 111

Nelson, A G. and Cohn, S. (2015). Data collection methods for evaluating museum programs and exhibitions, *Journal of Museum Education*, 40(1):27–36. DOI: 10.1080/10598650.2015.11510830. 121

Nissen, B., Bowers, J., Wright, P., Hook, J., and Newell, C. (2014). Volvelles, domes and wristbands: embedding digital fabrication within a visitor's trajectory of engagement. *Proceedings DIS'14*, New York: ACM, pp. 825–834. DOI: 10.1145/2598510.2598524. 60

Not, E. and Petrelli, D. (2018). Blending customisation, context-awareness and adaptivity for personalised tangible interaction in cultural heritage. *International Journal of Human-Computer Studies*, 114:3–19. https://www.sciencedirect.com/science/article/pii/S1071581918300016. DOI: 10.1016/j.ijhcs.2018.01.001. 26, 27

Not, E. and Petrelli, D. (2019). Empowering cultural heritage Pprofessionals with tools for authoring and deploying personalised visitor experiences, *User Modeling and User-Adapted Interaction*. Online first, DOI: 10.1007/s11257-019-09224-9. 98, 109

Not, E., Petrelli, D., Sarini, M., Stock, O., Strapparava, C., and Zancanaro, M.(1998). Technical note hypernavigation in the physical space: adapting presentations to the user and to the situational context. *New Review of Hypermedia and Multimedia*, 4(1):33–45. DOI: 10.1080/13614569808914694. 26

Obrist, M. (2017). Mastering the senses in HCI: Toward multisensory interfaces. *CHItaly '17 Proceedings of the 12th Biannual Conference on Italian SIGCHI Chapter*, Article 2. DOI: 10.1145/3125571.3125603. 54

Oh, H., Deshmane, A., Li, F., Han, J. Y., Stewart, M., Tsai, M., Xu, X., and Oakley, I. (2013). The digital dream lab, tabletop puzzle blocks for exploring programmatic concepts. *Proceedings of ACM TEI 2013*, New York: ACM, pp. 51–56. 22

O'Hara, K., Kindberg, T., Glancy, M., Baptista, L., Sukumaran, B., Kahana, G., and Rowbotham, J. (2007). Collecting and sharing location-based content on mobile phones in a zoo visitor experience. *Computer-Supported Cooperative Work*, 16(1-2):11–44. DOI: 10.1007/s10606-007-9039-2. 27, 28

Othman, M. K. (2012). *Measuring Visitors' Experiences with Mobile Guide Technology in Cultural Spaces*, The University of York: York, UK, 2012. 26

Palmquist, S. and Crowley, K. (2007). From teachers to testers: How parents talk to novice and expert children in a natural history museum. *Science Education* 91:783–804. DOI: 10.1002/sce.20215. 106, 118

Pannier, M., Hornecker, E., and Bertel, S. (2016). Can't touch this – The design case study of a museum installation. In Prinz, W., Borchers, J., and Jarke, M. (eds.), *Mensch und Computer 2016 - Tagungsband*. Aachen: Gesellschaft für Informatik e.V. GI Digital Library. 14, 100

Patel, M., Heath, C., Luff, P., vom Lehn, D., and Cleverly, J. (2015). Playing with words: creativity and interaction in museums and galleries. *Museum Management and Curatorship*, 31(1):69–86. DOI: 10.1080/09647775.2015.1102641. 71, 119

Parry, R. (2013). The end of the beginning: Normativity in the postdigital museum, *Museum Worlds: Advances in Research*, 1:24–39. 123

Pekarik, A. J., Doering, Z. D., and Karns, D. A. (1999). Exploring satisfying experiences in museums. *Curator: The Museum Journal* 42(2). DOI: 10.1111/j.2151-6952.1999.tb01137.x. 7, 112, 119

Pekarik, A. J., Schreiber, J. B., Hanemann, N., Richmond, R., and Mogel, B. (2014). IPOP: A theory of experience preference. *Curator: The Museum Journal* 57(1):5–28. DOI: 10.1111/cura.12048. 7, 107

Perry, D. L. (2012). *What makes Learning Fun? Principles for the Design of Intrinsically Motivating Museum Exhibits*. Altamira Press. 1, 7, 9, 10, 120, 121

Pescarin, S. (2014). Museums and virtual museums in Europe: Reaching expectations. *SCIRES-IT-SCIentific RESearch and Information Technology*, 1(1):131–140. 44

Petrelli, D., Ciolfi, L., van Dijk, D., Hornecker, E., Not, E., and Schmidt, A. (2013). Integrating material and digital: A new way for cultural heritage. *ACM Interactions*, 20(4):58–63. DOI: 10.1145/2486227.2486239. 26, 91, 94, 95

Petrelli, D., Marshall, M. T.,O'Brien, S., McEntaggart, P., and Gwilt, I. (2017). Tangible data souvenirs as a bridge between a physical museum visit and online digital experience. *Personal and Ubiquitous Computing*, 21(2): 281–295. DOI: 10.1007/s00779-016-0993-x. 59, 110

Petrelli, D. and O'Brien, S. (2018). Phone vs. tangible in museums: A comparative study. *Proceedings of the CHI 2018 Conference on Human Factors in Computing Systems*. New York: ACM. DOI: 10.1145/3173574.3173686. 38

Pisetti, A., Not, E., and Petrelli, D. (2018). War at your doorstep: supporting communities discovering their local history via interactive technology. In Ciolfi, L., Damala, A., Hornecker, E., Lechner, M., and Maye, L. (eds.) *Cultural Heritage Communities: Technologies and Challenges*, London and New York: Routledge, pp. 185–201. 38

Pitsch, K., Wrede, S., Seele, J.-C., and Süssenbach, L. (2011). Attitude of German museum visitors toward an interactive art guide robot. *HRI'11 Proceedings of the 6th International Conference on Human-Robot Interaction*, New York: ACM, pp. 227–228 https://dl.acm.org/citation.cfm?id=1957744. 111

Pujol-Tost, L.(2011). Integrating ICT in exhibitions. *Museum Management and Curatorship*, 26(1):63–79. DOI: 10.1080/09647775.2011.540127. 39

Pujol-Tost, L. and Economou, M. (2007). Exploring the suitability of virtual reality interactivity for exhibitions through an integrated evaluation: the case of the Ename Museum. *Museology*, 4:81–97. 45

Reunanen, M., Díaz, L., and Horttana, T. (2015). A holistic user-centred approach to immersive digital cultural heritage installations: Case Vrouw Maria. *Journal on Computing and Cultural Heritage*, 7(4), Article 24. DOI: 10.1145/2637485. 88

Reussner, E. M. (2010). *Publikumsforschung für Museen: Internationale Erfolgsbeispiele*. Bielefeld: Transcript Verlag. 14

Ridel, B., Reuter, P., Laviole, J., Mellado, N., Couture, N., and Granier, X. (2014). The revealing flashlight: Interactive spatial augmented reality for detail exploration of cultural heritage artifacts. *Journal on Computing and Cultural Heritage,* 7(2), Article 6. DOI: 10.1145/2611376. 49. 50

Ridge, M. (2014). *Crowdsourcing Our Cultural Heritage*. London: Ashgate. 76, 77, 79

Risseeuw, M., Cavada, D., Not, E., Zancanaro, M., Marshall, M., Petrelli, D., and Kubitza, T. (2016). An authoring environment for smart objects in museums: the meSch approach. In Ardito, C., Bellucci, A.,Desolda, G., Divitini, M., and Mora, S. (eds.) *Smart Ecosystems creation by Visual Design 2016*. CEUR-WS, pp. 25–30. 98

Roberts, J., and Lyons, L. (2017). The value of learning talk: Applying a novel dialogue scoring method to form interaction design in an open-ended, embodied museum exhibit. *International Journal of Computer-Supported Collaborative Learning*, 12(4):343–376. DOI: 10.1007/s11412-017-9262-x. 42, 120

Roozenburg, M. (2013). Smart replicas: bringing heritage back to life. In *Smart Replicas*, The Hague: Royal Academy of Art, pp. 28–31. 38

Roussou, M. (2000). Immersive interactive virtual reality and informal education. *Proceedings of User Interfaces for All: I3 Spring Days, 2000*. https://www.academia.edu/635273/Immersive_interactive_virtual_reality_in_the_museum. 43

Roussou, M. and Katifori, A. (2018). Flow, staging, wayfinding, personalization: Evaluating user experience with mobile Mmuseum narratives. *Multimodal Technologies and Interaction*, 2(2):32. DOI: 10.3390/mti2020032. 28

Roussou, M., Pujol, L., Katifori, A., Chrysanthi, A., Perry, S., and Vayanou, M. (2015). The museum as digital storyteller: Collaborative participatory creation of interactive digital experiences. *Proceedings of MW2015: Museums and the Web 2015*. 49

Roussou, M., Kavalieratou, E., and Doulgeridis, M. (2007). Children designers in the museum: applying participatory design for the development of an art education program. In *Proceedings of the 6th International Conference on Interaction Design and Children (IDC '07)*, New York: ACM, pp. 77–80. DOI: 10.1145/1297277.1297292. 91

Russo, A. (2011). Transformations in cultural communication: Social media, cultural exchange, and creative connections. *Curator: The Museum Journal*, 54(3):327–346. DOI: 10.1111/j.2151-6952.2011.00095.x. 75, 78

Salgado, M. (2008). The aesthetic of participative design pieces: Two case studies in museums. *International Journal of the Inclusive Museum*, 1(1):105–110. DOI: 10.18848/1835-2014/CGP/v01i01/44262. 73, 81

Salgado, M. and Díaz-Kommonen, L. (2006). Visitors' voices. In Trant, J. and Bearman, D. (Eds.). *Proceedings of the Museums and the Web 2006. Toronto: Archives and Museum Informatics*. http://www.archimuse.com/mw2006/papers/salgado/salgado.html. 72

Salgado, M., Saad-Sulonen, J., and Diaz, L. (2009). Using on-line maps for community-generated content in the museums. In J. Trant and D. Bearman (Eds.) *Proceedings of the Museums and the Web 2009*. Toronto: Archives and Museum Informatics. http://www.archimuse.com/mw2009/papers/salgado/salgado.html. 73, 75

Samis, P. (2018). Revisiting the Utopian promise of interpretive media. In Drotner, K.,Dziekan, V., Parry, R., and Schrøder, K. M. (eds), *The Routledge Handbook of Museums, Media and Communication*. London: Routledge, pp. 47–66. DOI: 10.4324/9781315560168-5. 123

Samis, P. and Michaelson, M. (2016). *Creating the Visitor-Centred Museum*. London: Routledge. DOI: 10.4324/9781315531014. 8

Sandell, R. and Nightingale, E. (2012). *Museums, Equality and Social Justice*. London: Routledge. 2

Sandifer, C. (2003). Technological novelty and open- endedness: Two characteristics of interactive exhibits that contribute to the holding of visitor attention in a science museum. *Journal of Research in Science Teaching*. 40(2):121–137. DOI: 10.1002/tea.10068. 3

Sanford, C., Knutson, K., and Crowley, K. (2007). We always spend time together on sundays: How grandparents and their grandchildren think about and use informal learning spaces. *Visitor Studies* 10(2):136–151. DOI: 10.1080/10645570701585129. 9

Sanford, C. (2010). Evaluating family interactions to inform exhibit design: Comparing three different learning behaviours in a museum setting, *Visitor Studies*, 13(1):67–89. DOI: 10.1080/10645571003618782. 120

Schavemaker, M., Wils, H., Stork, P., and Pondaag, E.(2011). Augmented reality and the museum experience. *Proceedings of Museums and the Web 2011*. https://www.museumsandtheweb.com/mw2011/papers/augmented_reality_and_the_museum_experience. 46, 49

Schnädelbach, H., Koleva, B., Flintham, M., Fraser, M., Izadi, S., Chandler, P., Foster, M., Benford, S., Greenhalgh, C., and Rodden, T. (2002). The Augurscope: A mixed-reality interface for outdoors. *CHI '02 Proceedings of the SIGCHI Conference on Human Factors in Computing Systems*, New York:ACM, pp. 9–16. DOI: 10.1145/503376.503379. 52

Schnädelbach, H., Koleva, B., Paxton, M., Twidale, M., Benford, S., and Anastasi, R. (2006). The Augurscope: Refining its design. *Presence: Teleoperators and Virtual Environments*, 15(3):pp. 278–293. DOI: 10.1162/pres.15.3.278. 52

Schultz, M. K. (2013). A case study on the appropriateness of using quick response (QR) codes in libraries and museums. *Library and Information Science Research*, 35(3):207–215. DOI: 10.1016/j.lisr.2013.03.002. 24

Serrell, B. (1997). Paying attention: The duration and allocation of visitors' time in museum exhibitions. *Curator – The Museum Journal*. 40(2):109–125. DOI: 10.1111/j.2151-6952.1997.tb01292.x. 8, 27

Serrell, B. and Raphling, B. (1992). Computers on the exhibit floor. *Curator – The Museum Journal*, 35(3):181–189. DOI: 10.1111/j.2151-6952.1992.tb00753.x. 17

Sforza, F., Scagliarini, D., Coralini, A., Vecchietti, E., Cinotti, T.S., Roffia, L., Galasso, S., Malavasi, M., Pigozzi, M., and Romagnoli, E. (2001). Exciting understanding in Pompeii through on-site parallel interaction with dual time virtual models. *Proceedings of the 2001 conference on Virtual Reality, Archeology, and Cultural Heritage*, New York: ACM Press, pp. 83–90. 46

Shaer, O. and Hornecker, E. (2010). Tangible user interfaces: Past, present and future directions. *Foundations and Trends in HCI* (FnT in HCI) 3(1-2):1–138. 34

Sharp, H., Preece, J., and Rogers., Y. (2019). *Interaction Design Beyond Human-Computer Interaction*. 5th ed., Wiley. 85

Shay, S. (2018). Challenging political agendas through indigenous media: Hawai'i and the promotion and protection of cultural heritage through the use of social media. In Ciolfi, L., Damala, A., Hornecker, E., Lechner, M. and Maye, L. (Eds), *Cultural Heritage Communities: Technologies and Challenges*, London: Routledge, pp 166–184. 78

Simarro Cabrera, J., Frutos, H.M., Stoica, A. G., Avouris, N., Dimitriadis, Y., Fiotakis, G., and Liveri, K.D. (2005). Mystery in the museum: collaborative learning activities using handheld devices. *Proceedings of Mobile HCI 2005*, New York: ACM, pp. 315–318. DOI: 10.1145/1085777.1085843. 27, 75

Simon, N. (2010). *The Participatory Museum*. Museum 2.0. http://www.participatorymuseum.org/. 65, 67

Simon, N. (2016). *The Art of Relevance*. Museum 2.0. http://www.artofrelevance.org/. 67

Smith, R. C. and Iversen, O. S. (2010). When the museum goes native, *ACM Interactions*, 18(5): 15–19. 91

Smith, R. C. and Iversen, O. S. (2014). Participatory heritage innovation: designing dialogic sites of engagement. *Digital Creativity*, 25(3):255–268. DOI: 10.1080/14626268.2014.904796. 74

Smørdal, O., Stuedahl, D., and Sem, I. (2014). Experimental zones: two cases of exploring frames of participation in a dialogic museum. *Digital Creativity*. 25(3):224–232. DOI: 10.1080/14626268.2014.904366. 75

Snibbe, S. and Raffle, H. (2009). Social immersive media. *Proceedings of ACM CHI 2009*. New York: ACM, pp. 1447–1456. DOI: 10.1145/1518701.1518920. 9, 40, 41

Soren, B. (2009). Museum experiences that change visitors. *Museum Management and Curatorship* 24(3):233–251. DOI: 10.1080/09647770903073060. 67

Sportun, S. (2014). The future landscape of 3D in museums. In Levent and Pascual-Leone (eds.) *The Multisensory Museum*. 56

Steier, R. (2014). Posing the question: Visitor posing as embodied interpretation in an art museum. *Mind, Culture and Activity*, 21:148–170, Routledge. DOI: 10.1080/10749039.2013.878361. 41

Stevenson, J. (1991). The long-term impact of interactive exhibits. *International Journal of Science Education*, 13(5):521–531. DOI: 10.1080/0950069910130503. 57

Stock, O. and Zancanaro, M. (2007). *PEACH - Intelligent Interfaces for Museum Visits*. London: Springer. DOI: 10.1007/3-540-68755-6. 26

Sylaiou, S., Economou, M., Karoulis, A., and White, M. (2008). The evaluation of ARCO: a lesson in curatorial competence and intuition with new technology. *Computers in Entertainment (CIE) - Theoretical and Practical Computer Applications in Entertainment*, 6(2) Article 23. 95, 96

Tallon, L. and Walker, K. (2008). *Digital Technologies and the Museum Experience*. AltaMira Press. 65

Taxén, G. (2004). Introducing participatory design in museums. *Proceedings of the Eighth Conference on Participatory Design: Artful Integration: Interweaving Media, Materials and Practices - Volume 1* (PDC '04), pp. 204–213. DOI: 10.1145/1011870.1011894. 91

Taylor, R., Bowers, J., Nissen, B., Wood, G., Chaudhry, Q., Wright, P., Bruce, L., Glynn, S., Mallinson, H., and Bearpark, R. (2015). Making magic: Designing for open interactions in museum settings. *Proceedings of ACM Creativity and Cognition 2015*, New York: ACM, pp. 313–322 . DOI: 10.1145/2757226.2757241. 32

Torpus, J. (2018). Extending museum exhibits by embedded media content for an embodied interaction experience. *Proceedings of the 10th Nordic Conference on Human-Computer Interaction (NordiCHI '18)*. New York: ACM, pp. 236–246. DOI: 10.1145/3240167.3240169. 51, 86, 88

Tsichritzis, D. and Gibbs, S. (1991). Virtual museums and virtual realities. *ICHIM 1991, International Conference on Hypermedia and Interactivity in Museums*. http://citeseerx.ist.psu.edu/viewdoc/download?doi=10.1.1.478.4705&rep=rep1&type=pdf. 43

Turchi, T. and Malizia, A. (2015). Pervasive displays in the wild: Employing end user programming in adaption and re-purposing. *IS-EUD 2015*, pp. 223–229. DOI: 10.1007/978-3-319-18425-8_20.

Vaucelle, C., Gorman, M.J., Clancy, A., and Tangney, B. (2005). Re-thinking real time video making for the museum exhibition space. *Proceedings of ACM SIGGRAPH 2005*. Article 24. New York: ACM Press. DOI: 10.1145/1186954.1186981. 69

Vayanou, M., Katifori, A., Karvounis, M., Kourtis, V., Kyriakidi, M., Roussou, M., Tsangaris, M., Ioannidis, Y., Balet, O., Prados, T., Keil, J., Engelke, T., and Pujol, L. (2014). Authoring personalised interactive museum stories. *International Conference on Interactive Digital Storytelling ICDS 2014: Interactive Storytelling*, pp. 37-48. 96

Vermeeren, A., Calvi, L., and Sabiescu, A. (2018). *Museum Experience Design. Crowds, Ecosystems and Novel Technologies*. London: Springer. DOI: 10.1007/978-3-319-58550-5. 65

Véron, E. and Levasseur, M. (1983). *Ethnographie de l'exposition: l'espace, le corps et le sens*. Réédition 1991. Paris: Bibliothèque Publique d'Information, Centre Georges Pompidou 1983. 107

Vi, C.T., Ablart, D., Gatti, E., Velasco, C., and Obrist, M. (2017). Not just seeing, but also feeling art: Mid-air haptic experiences integrated in a multisensory art exhibition. *International Journal of Human-Computer Studies*, 108:1–14. DOI: 10.1016/j.ijhcs.2017.06.004. 57

Vines, J., Clarke, R., Wright, P., McCarthy, J., and Olivier, P. (2013). Configuring participation: on how we involve people in design. *Proceedings of the SIGCHI Conference on Human Factors in Computing Systems (CHI '13)*, New York: ACM, pp. 429–438. DOI: 10.1145/2470654.2470716. 91

Vlahakis, V., Demiris, A., Bounos, E., and Ioannidis, N. (2004). A novel approach to context sensitive guided e-tours in cultural sites: Light augmented reality on PDA's. *VAST 2004, 5th International Symposium on Virtual Reality, Archaeology and Intelligent Cultural Heritage*, pp. 57–66. 46

Wakkary, R., Hatala, M., Muise, K., Tanenbaum, K., Corness, G., Mohabbati, B., and Budd, J. (2009). Kurio: a museum guide for families. *Proceedings of Conference on Tangible and Embedded Interaction (TEI '09)*, New York: ACM, pp. 215–222. DOI: 10.1145/1517664.1517712. 38

Walker, K. (2008). Structuring visitor participation. In L. Tallon and K. Walker (eds.) *Digital Technologies and the Museum Experience: Handheld Guides and Other Media*. Altamira Press. 81

Wein, L. (2014). Visual recognition in museum guide apps: do visitors want it? *Proceedings of the SIGCHI Conference on Human Factors in Computing Systems (CHI '14)*, New York: ACM, pp. 635–638. http://dl.acm.org/citation.cfm?doid=2556288.2557270. 24

West, R.M. (2004). The economics of interactivity. *Curator*, 47(2):213–223. DOI: 10.1111/j.2151-6952.2004.tb00118.x. 13

Weal, M. J., Hornecker, E., Cruickshank, D. G., Michaelides, D. T., Millard, D. E., Halloran, J., De Roure, D. C., and Fitzpatrick, G. (2006). Requirements for in-situ authoring of location based experiences. *Proceedings of the 8th Conference on Human-computer Interaction with Mobile Devices and Services* (MobileHCI '06), New York: ACM,pp. 121–128. DOI: 10.1145/1152215.1152241. 29, 96

Weilenmann, A., Hillman, T., and Jungseliu, B. (2013). Instagram at the museum: communicating the museum experience through social photo sharing. In *Proceedings of CHI '13. ACM*, NY, pp. 1843–1852. DOI: 10.1145/2470654.2466243. 27, 76, 112, 119

Wilson, P. F., Stott, J., Warnett, J. M., Attridge, A., Smith, M. P., and Williams,M. A., Warwick Manufacturing Group (WMG). (2018). Museum visitor preference for the physical properties of 3D printed replicas. *Journal of Cultural Heritage*. 32:176–185. DOI: 10.1016/j.culher.2018.02.002. 111

Wohl, J. (2016). Want to rent Van Gogh's 'bedroom'? *AdAge Magazine*. https://adage.com/article/creativity/art-instti/303425/. 76

Woods, E., Billinghurst, M., Aldridge, G., Garrie, B., and Nelles, C. (2004). Augmenting the science centre and museum experience. *Proceedings of the 2nd International Conference on Computer Graphics and Interactive Techniques in Australasia and South East Asia*, pp. 230–236. DOI: 10.1145/988834.988873. 47

Yalowitz, S. S. and Bronnenkant, K. (2009). Timing and tracking: Unlocking visitor behaviour. *Visitor Studies*, 12:1. DOI: 10.1080/10645570902769134. 103, 106, 107

Yoshino, K., Obata, K., and Tokuhis, S. (2017). FLIPPIN': Exploring a paper-based book UI design in a public space. *Proceedings of the 2017 CHI Conference on Human Factors in Computing Systems (CHI '17)*. New York: ACM, pp. 1508–1517. DOI: 10.1145/3025453.3025981. 36

Authors' Biographies

Eva Hornecker is a Professor of Human-Computer Interaction at the Department of Computing in the Faculty of Media at Bauhaus-Universität Weimar in Germany, with a second affiliation in the Faculty of Arts and Design. She holds a Doctorate (Dr.Ing) from the University of Bremen. Her work focuses on the human interaction angle of novel technologies beyond the desktop computer, in particular on tangible and full-body interaction and the user experience thereof, on social and situated interaction, and on how to design for these. Her work creates a bridge between technology, design, and social sciences. She is an expert on museum technology and the study of visitor interaction with installations, and in her research she has collaborated with museums in Germany, Austria, the UK, and the Netherlands. Eva is a Senior Member of the ACM and co-founded the ACM Conference on Tangible, Embedded, and Embodied Interaction (TEI).

Luigina Ciolfi is Professor of Human Centred Computing in the Faculty of Science, Technology and Arts at Sheffield Hallam University (UK). She holds a Ph.D. in Computer Science/Human-Computer Interaction from the University of Limerick. An active researcher and teacher in HCI and CSCW for over two decades in Italy, Ireland, and the UK, Luigina studies and writes about situated interaction, participation in design, and human practices in socio-technical settings. She has extensive experience with digital technologies for heritage, with a track record of projects involving national and European collaborators from academia, industry, and the cultural sector. She is an expert reviewer and advisor on these topics for several public funding bodies. Notable service roles include Associate Editor, *CSCW Journal*; Conference Chair, ECSCW 2017; Subcommittee Co-Chair, ACM CHI 2018-2019; and Papers Co-Chair, CSCW 2015. Luigina is a Senior Member of the ACM.

Printed in the United States
by Baker & Taylor Publisher Services